Hoodoo

Unlocking the Secret Power of Rootwork, Folk Magic, Conjuration, Witchcraft, and Mojo

Your Free Gift (only available for a limited time)

Thanks for getting this book! If you want to learn more about various spirituality topics, then join Mari Silva's community and get a free guided meditation MP3 for awakening your third eye. This guided meditation mp3 is designed to open and strengthen ones third eye so you can experience a higher state of consciousness. Simply visit the link below the image to get started.

https://spiritualityspot.com/meditation

Contents

Introduction

Hoodoo is a subject that has been around since Africans were brought to the American shores as slaves and migrated across the country, sharing their magic and beliefs. The herbs and roots they used were amalgamated with other beliefs to form the practice we now know as Hoodoo.

Many people think that Hoodoo is a religious practice, but the truth is quite the opposite. Hoodoo isn't based on worshipping Gods, Goddesses, or other formal deities. Instead, it is a way for people to practice folk magic using the most basic tools and ingredients. So, what relevance does Hoodoo have in today's society? Quite a lot! Humans are starting to understand just what powers lie in nature and how to use them.

The natural progression to magic and rootworking rituals passed down in history seems inevitable. Understanding why some plants and herbs can attract good luck while others form a protective shield appeals to our personal sense of well-being. This type of magic and conjuring can be carried out by anyone who wants to try it, providing you respect the power and learn how to protect yourself from harm.

This book has everything you need to know to perform the craft safely and powerfully. Learn the ancient craft of Hoodoo and see how it can change your life forever!

Chapter 1: A History of Hoodoo

Hoodoo was a practice used by African slaves to retain their roots when they were transported to the Americas as slaves. Hoodoo is folk magic and incorporates the beliefs and systems of ancient African cultures alongside the Christianity that slave masters insisted were taught to their slaves. It is not a religion, although it does have its own set of deities and gods you can worship or not, depending on your preferences.

Several sources say that Hoodoo is primarily an African-based system of protection and rootwork used to guard black people against their oppressors, and it should be practiced only by Black people. More modern practitioners believe there are three different threads of Hoodoo that encompass different ethnicities. There is a Black thread of Hoodoo for people with African heritage, a White thread for European influences, and a Red thread for Native Americans. However, all humans need to be acknowledged, and their differences celebrated for the rich tapestry of Hoodoo to be seen in its entirety.

Hoodoo is a personal practice and will be used in varying ways by different people. Cultural and theological influences will influence how individuals use the rituals and rootwork to protect or enrich their lives. Ancestor veneration is a core part of Hoodoo, and the work performed is often based on historical practices.

There are no barriers to Hoodoo. People may use it to cause harm and mischief, but mostly it is used to heal and protect. The work and rituals are influenced by certain materials and talismans to signal the intentions and needs of the person performing them. A knowledge of herbs and plants and the powers they represent is essential because when it's combined with other magical elements, it works in conjunction with them.

The origins of the term hoodoo are widely disputed, but it is thought to have originated in the 17th century with the arrival of enslaved African men and women in America. During the period of slavery in the US, people from multiple ethnic groups were thrown together to work for their white masters. These included people from the Kongo, Akan, and Ewe, among many other places. These people brought with them their indigenous knowledge and beliefs that melded together to become the practice of Hoodoo.

The extent to which the slaves could practice their folk magic depended on the tolerance of their slave owners, and some regions practiced freely while others were forced to take the practice underground. A melee of beliefs and practices became the basis for this magic, and Hoodoo was used to heal and protect the slaves from their masters and bring misfortune to those that mistreated them.

What is Voodoo?

The main difference between Hoodoo and Voodoo is that Voodoo is a religion. It has specific practices, and religious leaders are required to undergo some form of ordination. In Hoodoo, there is no such formality, and everyone is free to perform the rites and rootwork that form the magical aspect of the tradition.

Voodoo has two distinct branches known as Haitian Voodoo and Louisiana or New Orleans Voodoo. There are different spellings of the word, including Vodoun or Vodou, and the two branches follow distinctly different influences.

Haitian Vodou is an African religion that traveled from the island of Haiti when members of the tribes from that area were transported into slavery and developed bonds to ensure they could depend on one another under those horrific conditions. The Lwa spirits became a focal point that all the members turned to for guidance. These included the Gede Lwa, who represented the spirits of the dead, and the Petwo Lwa, who embodied the fiery spirit of the Congo. The rituals and spells they performed involved gris-gris and magic wanga, and their liturgical language was Kreyol.

Louisiana Vodoun is distinctly different. It draws on an amalgamation of religious practices with deep spiritual roots. It shares many roots with Hoodoo but shouldn't be confused with the practice. This form of Voodoo mixes the traditional Lwa spirits of traditional Haitian Voodoo with Catholic saints and symbolism. The liturgical language used by practitioners was English with a smattering of French Creole.

Both forms of Voodoo used veves (religious symbols) and other ornately painted symbols to decorate their surroundings using cornmeal and sand to draw them on the floor. All these symbols have meaning and are related to Saints. Followers could leave offerings to the Lwa family and the related Catholic Saint on designated holidays. These veves are used to create a bridge between the spiritual and physical worlds, and when used in rituals, the participants are inviting the Lwa to take possession of their bodies for transportation purposes.

Unfortunately, racist stereotype depictions of Voodoo practices in movies and television have given both these practices a bad name. Using voodoo dolls or puppets to harm people and the casting of spells to zombify people are far from the truth. Satan doesn't play a part in Hoodoo or Voodoo. There are no pacts with the devil and no shrinking heads. Using magic dolls to cause harm to people is a European witchcraft tradition.

Hoodoo is Southern folk magic and is primarily concerned with healing and improving certain aspects of life. Healing powders and magical baths are enhanced with candles and lamps to perform spell work. These rituals are often accompanied by prayers and readings from the Bible while invoking the spirits of the Catholic saints. This type of petitioning is more personal and doesn't involve imagery or rituals.

Hoodoos Conjure Doctors and Spiritual Mothers Through the Ages

The best way to show how Hoodoo has been practiced through the years is to study some of the more famous examples of doctors or rootworkers from history.

Every rural community had a conjure doctor responsible for healing and had an ancestral knowledge of herbs, roots, and bones. They would have a bag of tricks filled with a mixture of natural and human-made items that could influence health, wealth, and prosperity. They also had the power to bring retribution to people who harmed others, which came in the form of illness or bad luck.

Historical records indicate that these types of hoodoo practitioners were born with the gift of spiritual powers and were often blessed with the gift of sight. This meant they could foretell the future and could give advice about all aspects of life. Several people believed that babies born with a caul over their head (or seventh sons or daughters) possessed certain powers.

Most conjure doctors or rootworkers inherited their powers or had them passed down through the generations. Not everybody welcomed these powers, and many saw them as a blight on their lives. There is a report of an individual named Henry Barnes, who was born in 1858 in Alabama, being born with the power of a discerning eye which meant he could see spirits. His mother decided this was a curse when her son reported seeing a cow with no head, and she set about removing his abilities. She forced her son to stir the lard when she was rendering it because she believed that cured the power of sight. Henry wrote that after stirring the lard, he didn't see spirits anymore.

Aunt Caroline Dye

Possibly the best-known sightseer of the nineteenth century, her birth name was Caroline Tracy, born in 1843 and married to her husband Martin Dye in 1867. Her legend describes her as a hoodoo woman who was a two-headed doctor, a fortune teller, and a powerful conjurer.

She would hold sessions in her Newport home and dispensed her predictions, using just a deck of cards to help her readings. She refused to deal with matters of the heart, and later in her life, she also steered clear predictions about any war or conflict (She pointedly refused to speculate on the outcome of WW1.) Aunt Caroline's reputation grew as she helped locate missing people, livestock, and personal items. She would locate areas of land that would become successful farming ventures, and it was reported that prominent businessmen wouldn't make decisions without consulting her first.

Aunt Caroline never charged for her services, but it was an unwritten rule that people who benefitted from her help would leave a few dollars as appreciation. She also received up to thirty letters a day containing pleas for her help along with monetary payments. Due to the steady traffic of people to her home, she took advantage of the situation by selling meals from her house.

Her husband died in 1907 and was buried in Gum Grove cemetery in Newport. Caroline joined him 11 years later after a short illness, and reports indicate that huge amounts of cash were found in her home. Her legacy persists as she was mentioned in two popular songs by the famous Memphis blues player, W. Handy. He mentioned a gypsy woman in both the "St Louis Blues" in 1914 and the "Sundown Blues" written nine years later. The popular African American combo known as the Memphis Jug Band also wrote a song about her called the "Aunt Caroline Dyer Blues" in the late 1920s.

Gullah Jack

Also known as Gullah Jack Pritchard, he was an African conjurer who practiced Hoodoo to attract slaves to revolt against their white slave masters in the Vesey slave conspiracy of 1822. Vesey was a carpenter and a prominent African American leader in South Carolina. He was sold as a boy into slave-hood and traveled the world with his master, Joseph Vesey. He became knowledgeable and educated, which meant he was held in regard by many of the slaves in the area.

Gullah Jack also had a reputation for leadership, and he armed the slaves with magical charms that would protect them from the buckra, the African name for white people. Pritchard and Vesey plotted to overthrow the state armory and arm local slaves to kill the white population of the city, steal their ships and return to their homelands, where slaves had already overthrown the government and where slaves now ruled.

It is easy to understand how appealing such a plot must have seemed to the slave population. Vesey had filled their heads with tales of overseas travel, and the power of his preaching combined with Pritchard's magic hoodoo powers and charms provided a heady combination for many. However, not all the slaves were loyal, and many leaked details of the revolt to their masters. Vesey, Gullah Jack, and numerous other conspirators were tried, found guilty, and subsequently hanged in July 1822.

Doctor Jim Jordan

A more recent hoodoo practitioner, James Spurgeon Jordan, was born in June 1871 and was a famous Hoodoo doctor from Como, North Carolina. He spent his whole life in his birthplace and garnered a reputation as a root doctor, gummer doctor, and all-around faith healer. In the 1890s, he began treating people with a range of diverse illnesses and was dismissed as a "trick doctor" because of his use of hoodoo imagery to impress his patients.

As his patients continued to get well, his reputation grew. Regular medical professionals and law enforcement authorities began to regard him with admiration, and he became known as an honest conjure doctor who treated his clientele with respect. He never charged for his services unless his powers had been effective and his patients were cured.

His kind disposition helped the teachings of Hoodoo become more accepted well into the 20th century. Dr. Jordan's practice underwent many significant changes during its 70-year span, and he became known for his ability to lift the shadows of ignorance and embrace the enlightened use of spiritual healing.

What Role Does Hoodoo Play in Modern Society?

Currently, we are more open to exploring spiritualism and new exciting magical avenues. We have the technology to explore different cultures and examine their teachings and beliefs. We all know how shamanism, Wicca, witchcraft and modern-day paganism, and Norse religions have risen in popularity, so surely Hoodoo can do the same.

Modern-day practitioners can embrace elements from across the world and fuse them with cultural influences depending on their location. They can take classes online and access forces to improve their lives in many ways, including monetary, health, love, and career improvements. They can also learn how to cast spells for revenge and retribution against those who have caused them harm.

The key to learning Hoodoo is to respect its history and understand the devastating foundations it came from. There was violence in the past, but that doesn't mean it can't be used for healthier outcomes in today's society. Improving your life is a powerful mission to undertake, and any form of magical or spiritual help you can gain will prove positive.

There has been a revival in the belief, thanks to people like Zora Hurston and Harry Hyatt, who worked together to preserve the beliefs and practices of Hoodoo. This led to a revival in the popularity of rootwork and magical spirituality in the early 1990s. Many modern writers have produced informative works about Hoodoo, including the popular publication Hoodoo and Conjure Quarterly, a journal describing Hoodoo and Folk Magic. Published in 2011, it is filled with historical and contemporary information about all types of magical practices and other forms of African Diaspora.

Chapter 2: Hoodoo Beliefs and Cosmology

Hoodoo is a truly eclectic form of beliefs that enables followers to embrace all forms of cultural teachings and higher beings. There are no rules, and practitioners can decide what form of Hoodooism they will practice.

Many core beliefs have turned the hodge-podge of magical practices into Hoodoo in today's recognizable form. These beliefs don't limit practitioners, but they just give them a core belief system to hold on to. They are still welcome to petition whichever higher being they choose, from the Sun god Ra to Papa Legba, as nobody judges who you choose to call on to remove obstacles and make life better.

Core Beliefs of Hoodoo Practitioners

• The Existence of Divine Providence

The common definition of Divine Providence is God. This is because traditional theism is based on a central figure that holds power over the universe. It tells us this divine being is responsible for all parts of creation. Hoodoo practitioners don't feel they need to follow a singular deity or a traditional idea of central power. It isn't unusual for Hoodoo followers to mix and match their deities to suit their needs. They can petition Jesus for protection in the morning while appealing to Ganesh for wisdom and call on the Mexican deity Santa Muertos to find them love.

- **Death is Not the End**

Rootworkers repeatedly call on their ancestors to help them with their daily lives, and they consult a higher plane to reach them. Hoodoo followers believe that when the physical body dies, the departed soul ascends to a higher plane to become an Ancestor. They can then be contacted by Earthbound relatives to consult with them as they offer their advice. They also intercede with the higher spirits on their behalf.

- **The Power of Clairvoyance**

The power of sight is one of the most powerful tools in a conjurer doctor's bag. The ability to see the future and communicate with disembodied spirits elevates their status in society. This form of power enables the individual to travel freely in the past and present to form a probable solution to the troubles happening in the present. The power of divination allows the participant to take an active part in others' lives and change circumstances to make the outcome better.

- **Doctrine of Signatures**

This concept is as old as mankind itself. Hoodoo teaches us there is a cosmic signature on everything in the world that indicates its intended use. Early practitioners would have to examine only a plant to understand what it should be used for.

Examples of How the Doctrine of Signatures Works

- Walnuts: These strange-looking nuts look like the human brain. Traditional healers believed that they were effective for treating head-related ailments and illnesses of the brain. Modern experts now know that the fatty acids in the nuts help improve concentration and aid memory function.

- Meadow Saffron: The roots of this plant look like a toe with gout. Incredibly, the bitter root has key ingredients like alkaloids used to treat the condition.

- Stinging nettles: The hairs on this plant look like the hairs on our heads. Traditional healers use nettles in lotions and creams to help improve blood circulation, resulting in improved hair growth. The hairs also look like animal stings, so the leaves are used to treat insect bites and stings.

- Lungwort: The white spots on this plant resemble the marks on diseased lungs, which is why the plant got its name. Healers have used it to treat tuberculosis and less dire lung conditions like coughs and asthma.

- **Retributive Justice**

Hoodoo practitioners are mainly focused on doing good and improving the lives of those around them. Most religions and practices embrace the philosophy of doing no harm to others, and no harm will befall you. Hoodoo differs, as it believes in the biblical principle of an "eye for an eye" and allows people to demand justice to fit the crime. This measured form of retribution will often take the form of inflicting illness and pain on the recipient but rarely involves more fatal outcomes.

- **Intention**

In certain belief systems, there is the power to curse and hex others, depending on the power of the person laying the curse. Hoodoo followers believe that such curses and jinxes will only work if the person they are directed at is deserving of the hex. Many Hoodoo practices involve powders labeled with intentions. These can include the following.

- Boss Fix powder designed to bring your boss into line

- Confusion powder designed to bring chaos to those working against you

- Court case powder is used to influence the judge and jury to find in your favor.

- Devils shoestring sachet used to restrain your enemies and restrict their movements.

- Hotfoot sachets to drive people from your life

For instance, the Boss Fix powder will only work on your boss and won't affect other people who work with you. Furthermore, it will only work if your boss is a bad one. If it doesn't work, then you may be a bad employee! The Court Case powder will only work for innocent parties and is not intended to get a favorable verdict for guilty parties.

This belief system stems from the Bible and, more specifically, Proverbs 26.2, which states, *"Like a fluttering sparrow or a darting swallow an undeserved curse will not come to rest."* Nobody receives a curse without reason, according to Hoodoo's beliefs.

One of the lesser-known influences in Hoodoo beliefs originates in Germany. The sixth and seventh Book of Moses has over 125 articles that can be used in magical practices. Hexenfoos listed in the books are powerful talismans and symbols that protect against even the most powerful forms of curses and hexes. They can be painted on cradles to protect babies and other household objects to protect the people who live there.

Legend tells of God dictating this detailed guide to witchcraft to Moses as he resided on Mount Sinai, but it was omitted from the Old Testament because of its power. The book's contents were then passed down through the ages until it reached King Solomon, who used the guide to become one of the most powerful figures in Christianity.

Immigrants brought German-language editions of this text to America, where it became part of Hoodoo legend. The traditional healers and conjure doctors of the early 19th century used the working spells and accompanying necromancy to enhance the rootwork they were using.

To summarize, Hoodoo has a set of principles that most of us would like to adhere to. Even if the magical aspects of the tradition don't appeal, the root beliefs might help you form a new set of intentions to adhere to.

What is the Spiritual Meaning of Stars?

The night skies have been a source of fascination since the beginning of time. The celestial bodies that twinkle above our heads were mysterious, and even with the knowledge we have today, they are still a source of wonder for humankind. Imagine how appealing the stars and planets must have looked to slaves who had no sense of freedom and were shackled to their work and masters.

It isn't surprising that, like many mythological, religious, and spiritual systems, the followers of Hoodoo looked to the cosmos to enhance their beliefs and connect with higher powers. Astrology and the connection to the stars begin with the term astrology. It is derived from two Greek words, Astron and logos, which translate as "a star" "that is said," which seems to suggest that the stars contain the word of God.

Astrology is not a mainstream technique used in Hoodoo. The phases of the moon and the signs of the Zodiac were often used to affect the timing of rootwork and other spells.

Intentions Dictated by Signs of the Zodiac

1) Aries: The house of self. The period of a new moon in Aries is all about changing yourself and your approach.

2) Taurus: The house of money. Now is the time to set intentions regarding wealth and income.

3) Gemini: The house of travel and commuting. Gemini is the perfect sign to begin new journeys. Start a new project and increase the chance of success by setting your intentions when the moon is in Gemini.

4) Cancer; The house of family. Set intentions to form stronger family bonds and contact people who have moved away or relocated. When the new moon is in Cancer, it's time to clean your house and get rid of clutter. Clear the physical space, and your mental strength will benefit.

5) Leo: The house of love. When the moon is in this sector, it's time to get those love potions working. Attract a new partner or starting a new project will work, and couples trying for a child will conceive more successfully during a new moon.

6) Virgo: The house of work. Intentions regarding your career or seeking new work will be auspicious in his period. This is also a good time to work on yourself, start a new health regime, and improve your diet and exercise routines.

7) Libra: The house of relationships. When the new moon is in the house of Libra, it signals the time to work on your connections. This includes your personal and business relationships. Try to strengthen the existing ties you may have neglected lately.

8) Scorpio: The house of an enigma. When the moon is in the eighth house, it's time to set intentions surrounding shared resources. Practical applications involve paying off debts and resolving tax issues so you can begin to start saving for future projects.

9) Sagittarius: The house of knowledge. This is an opportune time to expand your horizons and embrace new subjects. Take an online course about something that is completely outside your normal remit and would never have appealed to you before. Plan a trip to somewhere different, maybe swap a beach resort for more cultural breaks.

10) Capricorn: The house of the public. Now it's time to work on your image. This could mean updating your CV or improving your online presence. Be visible in the workplace, and you are receiving the recognition you deserve.

11) Aquarius: The house of friendship. Take the time and set intentions to meet new people. Network in different groups and increase your social interactions. This will help with work and personal life.

12) Pisces: The house of the hidden. Discover your inner self and use this time to meditate and find your inner peace. Set intentions to work on yourself and say no to other people. This is not a selfish outlook, and it just means you need to concentrate on nurturing yourself for once.

Hoodoo oils are especially connected to astrological timings. Using specific oils during the different phases of the moon will increase their effectiveness on the person using them.

While the Zodiac is important, other astral signs are also significant in the teachings of Hoodoo. The stars are one of the earliest forms of guidance, and Hoodoo's followers are no different. They represent divine energy that all people can direct their intentions toward. Their physical distance represents hard to achieve goals and reminds people they need to try harder and work toward their divine purposes. The symbolic meaning of the stars is complex and vast. They represent the powers of the divine beings and represent the concept of greatness and cosmic enlightening.

The Morning and the Evening Stars

While they have separate names, these two astral stars are actually the same celestial body. Because they were seen at different times, it was believed that they were two bodies and were named as such.

When the Morning Star rises, it leads the Sun into the sunrise and is seen as a leading light that brings knowledge and power. As the Sun sets in the evening, it can be seen shining brightly beside it before they both disappear behind the horizon. Many cultures believe this star is the embodiment of the fallen angel, Lucifer, whose name represents the personification of the light bringer.

Shooting Stars

Different cultures interpret falling stars in various ways. It can herald a change in fortune and an extremely positive omen or signal a fallen angel. Asian cultures see the appearance of a shooting star as a bad and negative omen, and Hoodoo followers interpret both meanings depending on the circumstances.

Solomon's Pentagram

Often the pentagram is associated with black magic and negative forces, but historically the opposite is true. Hoodoo followers have used this astral symbol to set intentions for generations. There are hundreds of combinations to promote blessings, love, and wealth and to punish wrongdoings. Combined with other pentacle signs and symbols, Solomon's pentagram is the ultimate sign of power and wisdom.

Modern practitioners will design their pentacles and pentagrams using traditional seals and symbols alongside more modern images.

A Brief Guide to Important Signs From Cosmology

- To enhance the power of the Sun, use a point within a circle
- A triangle is both a symbol of the Sun and the alchemic symbol of fire
- A crescent moon is a symbol for both the moon and water. This symbol will protect you from evil and bring good luck
- A triangle with a line across the base represents air
- The same triangle for air inverted represents the Earth

Using these basic symbols combined with other representations of your character and specifics will make your seal or symbol a true logo of your intentions.

Elements That Can be Included

- Your zodiac signs
- Your Chinese Zodiac signs
- Your preferred totem animals
- Your birthstones
- Favorite colors
- Preferred numbers
- Numerical birth number

The key to designing a logo that works in your Hoodoo practices is to have fun and just use the elements that appeal to you. The universe comprises amazing materials that will inspire you and fill your work with power.

Chapter 3: The Hoodoo Toolkit: Ingredients and Materials

Now it's time to get your hands dirty, literally! The Hoodoo practices and spells often include dirt and dust, which were readily available to all the practitioners no matter where they were. This type of ingredient is one of the most important hoodoo magic components and is known as *Goofer dust.*

What is Goofer Dust?

The name derives from the Bantu word kufua, which means "to die," and it is used to harm or kill the targeted victim. Composed primarily from graveyard dirt and dust, it also incorporates other ingredients depending on the required outcome. Snakeskin and salt are added to the dust to create a powerful way to cause someone harm.

The Goofer dust is spread on the victim's pillow or around the path they use to cause the greatest damage. The first sign the hex has worked is sharp pains in the legs or feet followed by severe swelling, which leads to the inability to walk. The term has also evolved to become a verb and a noun. The term "goofering someone" refers to any practice that involves a form of poisoning or inflicting harm by introducing injurious elements into their environment.

In January 2016, a man from Queens was sentenced to 50 years in prison for killing his parents five years earlier. After firing four sets of defense lawyers, he represented himself in court and claimed that his parents died as a direct result of his mother's use of goofer dust in the home. The truth was that he bludgeoned his mother to death and choked her with a pearl necklace before plunging her head into the bathtub.

Graveyard Dirt

Dirt and dust are different things. The dirt from graveyards is the actual soil surrounding the grave, while the dust is residual material found on the surface. The Bokongo people of Central Africa are believed to be the source of this form of magic, and they believed that the dirt contained the spirits of the people buried in the soil. When they traveled to America in 1730 as slaves, they brought this concept with them.

Graveyard dirt can't just be taken. It needs to be purchased. This involves communing with the dead person and creating a contract to buy the dirt. This would usually involve the purchaser leaving a gift on the grave for the deceased, usually in something they enjoyed in life, like liquor or money.

Not all graveyard dirt is equal. The dirt from the graves of babies and young children is especially powerful for healing and spells of good fortune, while the dirt from directly above the heart of the body is used for love spells. If you plan more iniquitous deeds, then the dirt from a murderer's grave will prove more powerful. Dirt from the graves of lesser criminals can be used to cast spells of chaos and disorder.

Plants and Herbs of Hoodoo

As with any form of witchcraft and magic, a major part of your toolkit will consist of natural materials like plants and herbs.

Here are a couple of the more powerful tools nature supplies for hoodoo magic:

- **The Rose of Jericho**

This is a Mexican plant that is also called the resurrection plant and the false plant. It is brown and brittle when dry, but when immersed in water, it unfurls and becomes a vibrant green sacred plant that is perfectly geometrical. Spells cast with this plant involve resurrecting an old love or creating love where there was none before.

- **Horsetail**

This verdant plant grows in humid environments and is known for its magical and medicinal properties. When harvested correctly, it is used to cleanse the body as it has beneficial fungicides, but it can be toxic if harvested at the wrong time.

- **Basil**

In Hoodoo, basil is used as a magnet of fortune. Adding this bright leafy herb makes a spell more powerful as a love potion or an inducement for prosperity. Basil can also be used to ward off evil spirits and bad vibes. More practically, it can help keep mosquitoes at bay.

- **John the Conqueror Root**

This is a staple part of Hoodoo rituals, and its powers can be traced back to early African American folklore. The story tells of the son of an African King named John the Conquer, who fell in love with the devil's daughter Lilith. The devil tried to trick John by setting him a task to win his daughter's hand, but John outwitted the devil and escaped to Africa with Lilith and the devil's magic horse.

It is this power of trickery and success that John is believed to have left behind in the Americas in this powerful root. You only have to possess the plant to benefit from the powers of luck and love it contains, and the essence of the root is used to bring power to candles, crystals, and sachets. Carry dried root with the hair of someone you love to draw their admiration and interest.

High John soaps and shower gels can refresh the body and build levels of confidence. They can also help you score on a hot date! You can make your own or buy them from commercial sites like luckshop.com who offer bars of soap for $5 that promise to raise your inner vibrations and strengthen your resolve.

- **Palo Santo**

This is one of the most powerful and sacred plants on Earth. Found in areas of South America, it is used to burn as a cleanser by shamans and other healers across the world. It can also be used to make herbal teas that will purify the body and improve the immune system. While it isn't commonly available, it can be sourced from traditional medicinal shops and apothecaries. It is available in resin, oil, or wood form and used as an essential oil to make fragrant steam.

- **Cinnamon**

This is an extremely useful, readily available part of your hoodoo tool kit. It is used for sexual arousal spells, and burning it when having sex is said to enhance the experience.

Cinnamon also attracts wealth, prosperity, and cleansing. Cinnamon tea is used to treat gastronomic problems and relieving sickness and vomiting. Cinnamon is often used as a protection tool when placed in doorways and windows in the home.

- **Plants Used to Attract Wealth**

There aren't many people who would turn down the chance to have more money or wealth, so many Hoodoo practices are centered on attracting wealth.

These plants will help your spells attract the prosperity you seek:

The money plant: Also known as the golden pothos, this plant should be placed around any sharp angles within the house to purify the home and make it a place for success.

The mother-in-law plant: Also known as the snake plant, this healthy plant provides a natural source of moisture and cleanliness.

Crassula: These vibrant plants have succulent leaves and are used to bring financial abundance to your home. They should be placed in the southeast corners of your home.

Bamboo: Asian cultures have used this plant for generations to bring good health and luck, and hoodoo practitioners have also embraced its qualities. Lucky bamboo is a genus of the plant used to bring blessings to you and your household.

Jasmine: The aroma this plant conjure attracts money and luck when placed around the home. It is also considered an aphrodisiac so that you can get rich and lucky simultaneously.

Sage: All good pagans know the power of sage and how it cleans and refreshes energy. Hoodoo is no different, and its healing properties are used to bring love and good luck to spells and potions.

Chamomile: This daisy-like plant is known for its calming effect and healing properties. When used in Hoodoo, it attracts wealth and power.

Bayberry: Grown in the East of the US, this is a shrub with dark bark and berries used to make medicine. When dried and blended, it attracts love and prosperity.

Hoodoo Tools

Actual tools have no magical powers without the spiritual intent of the user. They provide a medium to direct the spirituality and power that lies with the Hoodoo practitioner. Some people will find the powerful, while others will need just the barest essentials to practice their craft.

There is a wealth of choice when it comes to choosing your particular bag of tricks, and some items are fun to own even if they aren't used in magical rituals.

Amulets and Charms

These items are used to produce vibrations and energies for the holder and the recipient of magic. They often have daily functions, yet they become magical in the right hands. Candles and holders play a significant role in certain hoodoo rituals, and it is important to have a stock of them in various colors.

Many of the most effective amulets are formed by the user and contain personal effects like hair and nail clippings to give them extra power. There are several powerful talismans connected to luck, and that are carried by gamblers and poker players. Most of these contain symbols originating from the Key of Solomon and attract power, success, and wealth.

Coyote Claws

Coyotes are known for their trickster ways, and stories tell of them stealing fire from the gods to give it to mankind, setting his tail on fire during the raid, which accounts for the markings on their tail.

Although the coyote is a rogue, he has mankind's best interest at heart. He can travel in the dark and find water in desolate places. His claw is carried by scouts and travelers who want to benefit from his skills and remain undiscovered when traveling. Claws can be purchased from select online hoodoo suppliers.

Porcupine Needles

These American needles are fun to use and can be incorporated in candles, dolls, and rootwork. They provide protection and should be placed around the object that needs protecting with the black pointy bit facing outward.

Incense

Burning incense when performing spells and rituals enhances the experience and signals the intention of the practitioner. Use a clay burning bowl to burn your incense and self-igniting charcoal to fuel the flame.

Blends of Incense and What They Promote

- African juju: Used to draw passion and intense desire into a relationship.

- Banishing: Remove unwanted and harmful people from your life by burning this incense when casting your spells.

- Chuparosa: Also known as hummingbird incense, burn it to draw your lover closer like a hummingbird seeking nectar.

- Dragon's blood: Containing the real blood of dragons, this resin should be burned to bring power and strength when performing rituals.

- Has no Hanna: This incense should be used to enhance your tools. Pass them through the smoke to enhance, charge and reenergize them before use.

- Jinx killer: This special blend of incense is burned to give protection from all hexes and curses sent your way.

- Obeah: This incense is burned by sorcerers and rootworkers who wish to communicate with the spirits.

- Seven African Powers: This orisha essence is used to obtain energy from Africa's seven saints.

- Tranquility: Burned to bring peace and harmony to your home.

Lucky Hoodoo products Inc. creates and blends these incense products and many more. If you don't see the product you require, ask them to blend the formula to suit your needs. Prices range between $9 and $30 for 2 oz tins.

Crossing Products

Sometimes you need to take the gloves off and fight your enemies with powerful rootwork. You can use your herbs and other ingredients to blend your own formulas, or you can buy oils and powders ready-made from online sources.

Black Arts Oil

This is one of the most powerful blends in Hoodoo. It is used to cross up or curse your enemies who have caused harm to you or your loved ones. You can create your oil using baneful substances like snakeskin, red pepper, and sulfur mixed with the herbs you prefer, or you can buy ready mixed oil online.

Boss Fix Oil

When the hoodoo community wanted to "give it to the man" or give their boss a taste of their wrath, they would concoct a fixing oil or powder to cause discomfort when they touched certain objects like keys or doorknobs. Mixtures containing licorice, high john herbs, and other powerful herbs were used to pay back bosses who were less than kind to their staff.

This type of oil or powder can be used in modern workplaces and can be sprinkled onto their office doorknob or computer keyboard. Recite an accompanying prayer to stop them from micromanaging you and realize what a key worker you are.

Poppets

These traditional dolls are often mistaken for voodoo dolls that represent other people and that are used to cause pain. In hoodoo practices, poppets are formed from cloth or wax and represent a spirit connected to the owner. There is no malice intended when a poppet is formed, and if you treat your doll well, it will do the same for you.

When making your poppet, the color of the fabric you use will determine the powers it holds. They can be made from simple white felt and then added to, or you can choose a hue from the list below to imbue your poppet with magic:

Banishing: Black fabric decorated with swords or fire.

Ingenuity: Use orange or yellow fabrics with bright symbols like the sun or fire.

Healing: Use spiritual colors like pale blue or white and decorate with clouds and stars.

Love and passion: Red or deep pink fabric decorated with hearts and bows.

Wealth: Silver or gold fabric with green trims. Decorate with dollar bills or coins and cups.

Protection: Red or white material decorated with shields or keys. Use mistletoe to add an extra layer of protection.

Other Tools That Are Part of Hoodoo Lore

Lodestones

Naturally occurring magnetized pieces of iron ore lodestones are used to draw positive influences toward the user. They attract love and money and are also used to direct spells away from the practitioner who has been cast by others.

Lucky Blue Balls

Known as anil in Latin American countries, these bright blue spheres are made from copper sulfate and carried for good luck. When dissolved in water, they provide a cleansing solution that will protect your house and make it a lucky place to live.

Pyrite

Known as fool's gold, this shiny mineral is widely used in Hoodoo to draw money and success to the person who carries it. Small chunks of the material can be bought for as little as $10 and make a perfect accompaniment for important attraction spells.

Coins

Certain coins play roles in Hoodoo and are often silver dollars or souvenir good luck coins. These will often have a personal attachment to the person who carries them. In the 1930s, at the height of the Great Depression, these coins were manufactured to bring luck to people who were suffering. They feature horseshoes, four-leaf clover, and other symbols of good luck.

Most of the coins have no monetary value and can be found online or in traditional shops selling hoodoo paraphernalia.

Mojo Beans

Also known as wishing beans and African mojo beans, these are classic good luck talismans and should be carried in a piece of red material to bring the holder good fortune.

Twice Stricken Lightning Wood

This is a popular tool in Hoodoo and is a powder ground from wood that has been struck by lightning. It has powers of attraction that can be used for sexual spells and commanding a lover to return. It also has cleansing properties as the lightning represents the power of purity and transformation.

Bones

Throwing the bones is one of the most traditional forms of divination and is part of hoodoo-style worship. The bones used will all have a meaning, and how the throw is interpreted will depend on the person who casts them. The bone reader should cast a petition to the gods describing what they need to know before casting the bones to the mat or animal skin covering a table.

Many people believe that the further away the bones fall means they depict things from the future while the closest bones relate to the present. Spaces between the bones or the shapes they make all have relevance.

If you intend to perform this divination rite, it is important to have a variety of natural bones and other objects to cast. Include items like:

- The arm from a china doll
- Alligator foot
- Sharks' tooth
- Dog ankle bone
- Shell from nutmeg
- Snake vertebra
- Raccoon penis bone
- Rabbit rib bone
- Abalone shell
- Cowrie shell
- Vintage keys

- Ravens' claw

- Chickens' foot

This is just a selection of items you can use to throw the bones. Add jewelry or personal items to make the reading more relevant to whoever wants their questions answered.

Chapter 4: Spiritual Cleansing Basics

Your Hoodoo toolkit may seem like the most important part of your practical work, but you also need to keep your tools and home clean. They need to be physically clean, but more importantly, they – and you –should be spiritually clean.

The ingredients you need will differ depending on your requirements and methods, but there are some standard components in a Hoodoo cleansing kit. Spiritual cleansing is important for many reasons. It allows you to perform at your best, and it banishes any negative energies that may attach themselves to yourself and your environment. Think of these cleansing rituals as being the spiritual equivalent of washing your hands and brushing your teeth. They need to be done regularly and thoroughly.

What You Need to Have in Your Cleaning Kit

- Candles
- Salt
- Brick dust
- Graveyard dirt
- Chicken or turkey wing

- Chicken foot

- Crystals

- Herbs like sage, rosemary, sweetgrass, and palo santo

- Holy or blessed water

- Essential oils

- Natural bath salts

- Alcohol rub

Personal Cleansing

This form of ritual is especially important if you are feeling under the weather or anxious about something. If you feel like your powers are waning and you have blockages in your aura, then cleansing your body and soul will help you restore your energy levels.

Cleansing is one of the most important parts of conjure work, and it's essential to make time for your rituals. To get the best results to perform the cleansing during certain planetary hours. This will increase the powers of your ritual and give them added intentions. Use an online planetary hour calculator to calculate the body that rules the day and choose the best day for you.

Ritual baths are the perfect way to cleanse your aura and feel the power of your magic for hours after. If you feel that negative energies stop you from being yourself, draw a hot bath, add natural bath salts, drops of essential oil (citrus oils like lemongrass and ylang-ylang are perfect), add two cups of blessed water, and sprinkle with your favorite herbs. Light two white candles and place them at the side of your bath. Add the ingredients as the bath fills to energize the atmosphere, and when it is filled, step in.

Now take a jug and pour the water over your head 13 times while reciting a cleansing prayer. Psalm 37 is a prayer option, or you can compose your own prayer. Only wash downward, so negative energies are flushed into the bathwater. Once you feel refreshed and cleansed, step out of the bath, and air dry yourself (no drying with towels) before dressing in clean clothes. Now take a jug full of the bathwater before draining the rest. Take your saved bathwater and head for a crossroads. Throw the water over your shoulder and then walk back home without looking back. If you are lucky enough to have trees in your garden, you can dispose of the bathwater by throwing it at the trunk so it can absorb the negativity.

Handy tip: This type of bath can be used as an attraction bath with a few simple changes. Use the same ingredients but add rose petals or other floral essential oils to your water. Wash in an upward manner and pour the water over your head 7 or 9 times. Recite Psalm 23 or other uplifting text while you wash and then air dry yourself before dressing. Using yellow or red candles will make the object of your attraction more attainable, and the saved water should be used to wash your front doorstep and be swept inwards to bring the attraction toward you.

Quick-Fix Methods of Cleansing Yourself

If you can't use baths to cleanse yourself because you don't have the time, or you just need a quick fix, you can use several of the following methods to remove negativity.

The chicken foot: This is a wonderful tool for cleansing, and lightly scratching yourself with it will keep your energy positive and will remove any negative energies. Think how the chicken deals with its mess. It simply scratches it away and moves on!

Brushing: If you feel like your cleansing should be more rigorous, but you want to use natural elements, then upgrade to a turkey or chicken wing. If you feel the need to remove a crossing or a jinx, take the turkey wing and brush it down from the top of your head to the base of your feet. Traditionally turkeys gobble up all the mess, so the wing will remove the condition and cleanse your aura.

Rubdown

Use your alcohol rub to form a base. Add herbs and oils to infuse the mixture before rubbing yourself down. Perform the ritual in a sacred place and use prayers and spiritual chants to enhance the experience.

Candle Cleansing

Use a black candle to remove a crossed or jinxed condition. Wipe yourself with the candle in downward movements while praying.

Smoke Cleansing

Also known as smudging, this process can be performed by burning incense, essential oils, or dried herbs. Use a white cloth to cover yourself from the neck down and burn the selected items under it. Allow the smoke to swirl around you before removing the sheet and allowing the smoke to permeate the house.

Sprinkle

Use a sprinkler head to perform this ritual. Fill it with holy or blessed water and add salt and essential oils to the liquid. Sprinkle your head and shoulders with the water, recite your favorite psalm (psalm 23 works well), and then sprinkle your feet.

Cleansing and Blessing the Home

Floor washes based on the elements used in cleansing baths can be used to clean houses and other physical places. The same rule of directing energies applies to floor washes, just like it applies to bathing. Wash windows and doors downward to dispel negativity and upward to attract goods, luck, and wealth. Candles, prayers, and smudging can all be used to give your cleanse added depth.

Hoodoo practitioners will often use elemental ingredients to increase the power of their house cleanses and blessings. Here are a few ways to use these strong influences in your rituals:

Earth

Actual dirt is the most basic elemental form of Earth, but not everyone wants to have dirt on their floor. Several substitutes can be used just as effectively.

- Redbrick dust: Hoodoo practitioners believe this form of Earth is particularly effective, and they will sprinkle it almost everywhere. Doorways and windows, thresholds, and entrances should all be protected, and red brick dust does the job perfectly. The most powerful dust is from old houses or sacred buildings, and homemade dust can be found almost everywhere. There are specialist spiritual products online, but ensure they are reputable and the dust has provenance.

Lay unbroken lines across your thresholds to form psychic barriers that are impossible to cross. The most effective time to perform this ritual is the eve of the full moon, and the dust should be replaced monthly.

- Salt: Salt is readily available and can be removed only by evaporation. Sea salt is particularly effective, and many Hoodoo practitioners swear by the salt from the Dead Sea. Salt or saltwater can be used to solve problems with nightmares and bad dreams. Sprinkle the area around the bed with salt to remove nighttime influences and aid healthy sleep. A box filled with sea salt at your front door will protect your home and stop negative energy from entering.

- Black salt: This is a mixture of regular or sea salt with iron filings or charcoal. This type of salt should be used when obstructions or negative energies are particularly strong.

Air

This element is incorporated naturally in house blessings and cleanses. Burning candles or incense permeates the air while doors and windows can be opened to allow negativity to escape.

Fire

Both black and white candles bring power to your cleansing. Their potency is increased when combined with essential oils like Myrrh or Sandalwood. Use burners to protect and clean doorways and windows.

Water

Most deep cleanses are based around the element water, and it is used to wash away a multitude of ills. You can ask your local church for blessed water, or it can be purchased online.

Alternatively, You Can Bless Your Own Water With the Following Method

Step 1: Collect seawater for your cleanse. If you take it from natural sources, be sure to leave a gift for the spirits that live there. A small offering of fresh fruit or vegetables will show you are thankful for their blessings.

Step 2: Gather rainwater. Use open containers to collect fresh rainwater from your garden or windowsill. Water gathered during a thunderstorm is particularly effective. The morning dew is also used for rituals to bring revitalization to your home.

Step 3: Make your water holy

There are Hoodoo practitioners that believe in the power of moonlight, and leaving your water outside overnight renders it holy. Mix the seawater and rainwater and place the mix in a silver or glass container. Place the container on a table in the garden where it will receive the most exposure to moonlight. Charge the water with your blessings and prayers before you leave it.

Other practitioners believe that prayer is the most powerful way to create holy water. Use readings and prayers from your favored texts and religious teachings to bless your water. A simple way to do this is to say, *"Water is the giver of life, and I ask the powers of the spiritual world to bless it and make it holy. I call upon the Gods and Goddesses to infuse this water with love, purity, and peace."*

Step 4: Add salt

Ideally, you will use a form of holy salt. Use the same phrase as you did for the water but replace the phrase "giver of life" with "preserver of life" to consecrate your salt and make it more powerful.

Step 5: Combine the two elements. Add pinches of salt to the water while stirring in a clockwise direction. Say the final prayer, *"This holy union is blessed with the power of the elements and life. The Gods and Goddesses have made this union powerful and ready to be used in goodness and health."*

Cleansing Spells for Toxicity

The modern world is filled with sources of negative energy. The environment we occupy is prone to toxins and negativity, so sometimes we need to clear specific areas of frustration and negativity. These spells are designed to focus on intentions rather than perform a general cleansing ritual.

Moonlight Spell

You will need:

- Incense

- Calming music

- White candle

Step 1: On the evening of a full moon, take a cleansing bath before air-drying yourself and dressing in a white robe.

Step 2: Find a calm relaxing place outdoors or in front of a window that allows you to see the moon.

Step 3: Play your music and light your incense.

Step 4: Call upon the spirit who guards you, this can be a God or Goddess, or you can call on your angel you feel an affinity toward or your guardian angel.

Step 5: Ask them to protect your soul's energy and fill you with their healing powers.

Step 6: Feel the energy flow into you from the base of your feet to the top of your head.

Step 7: Forgive yourself for being human; feeling the pressures of the world begin to overcome your emotions.

Step 8: Thank the universe for its blessings and your individual angel or spirit for their help.

Spell for the Soul

If you feel that your soul is heavy and the world is taking over, regain your control by performing this powerful spell.

You will need:

- White candle
- Blessed water
- Holy salt
- Dried sage
- Bowl for burning herbs

Step 1: Choose a night during a waning moon to perform the ritual.

Step 2: Light the candle and invite the spirits to bless your endeavors.

Step 3: Quickly move your hand through the candle flame while reciting the following phrase *"I use this fire to release the negative energies within me, and I ask they are replaced with good intentions."*

Step 4: Rub the holy salt into your hands and say, *"Through this earthly element, I relinquish all obstacles and elements of negativity in my life."*

Step 5: Now burn your dried sage in the bowl. Breathe in the smoke and say, *"With the element Air, I cleanse my soul and remove all troubling thoughts."*

Step 6: Plunge your hands into the water and say, *"I use the element water to release my toxins and bring clear intentions to my soul."*

Now take the time to enjoy your newly charged soul and fill your thoughts with the future you will have.

Step 7: Dispose of the ingredients by mixing the salt with the ashes and dissolving it in the water. Bury the mixture at the base of a tree or scatter it at a crossroads.

These types of rituals are designed so you can customize them to suit your needs and requirements. Just like Hoodoo itself, the rituals and cleanses are made to be powerful extensions of your beliefs. If you have a strong bond with Catholicism, the holy water process will differ from the one described here. Listen to your heart and soul and be led by your instincts.

Chapter 5: Creating a Mojo Bag

One of the simplest ways to make your magic practices more effective and personally charged is by using a mojo bag to carry your charms and magical tools. They are also called gris-gris bags, toby, conjuring sacks, and condition bags.

You can have as many mojo bags as you like, and tailoring them to suit your needs is simple. Think of your mojo bags as batteries for your powers that need recharging regularly and should always be carried with you. There are many commercial types of bags available, but a handmade one will help you connect to your magical sources. Creating your bag is simple but satisfying, and the objects you place within them are paramount to the success of your intentions.

Hands-on involvement with ritual work enhances the power you create, so if you can hand sew the bag with colored thread and use decorative ribbon, you will be investing part of yourself into the bag. This will increase the effectiveness of its contents and lift the energy they emit.

Color is a major factor when choosing the fabric for your bags, but the material is also important. Rich velvets and satins work well for some, while others will prefer muslin or cotton materials. Remember, you know what suits you and what your bag will be used for. Treat your mojo bag as an extension of your character, and it will serve you well.

Colors to Choose for Your Mojo Bag

• Gold: This works with the Sun and encourages wealth and success combined with projectivity. The god yang is linked with gold, and he provides a loud, in-your-face type of energy.

• Silver: Working with the moon, the goddess yin is linked with this color and promotes meditative processes and peace.

• Red: Connected to the planet Mars, passion and courage are associated with this hue. The deeper the red, the more energetic the mojo.

• Orange: Associated with the planet Mercury, orange is the color of success. It helps give the ingredients of the bag the power of vitality and speed.

• Yellow: Governed by the Sun, yellow is the color of joy and creativity. Bring an aura of allure to your spells when you store your tools in this bag.

• Green: working with the planet Venus your bag will be imbued with the power of good fortune and wealth.

• Blue: Associated with the planet Jupiter use blue material to bring wisdom and rhetoric to your spells. This is the color of intelligence and represents the deep connection you have mentally with the spirits.

• Violet: This striking color is all about healing and aiding karmic connections. Tools kept in this bag will be powerful when connecting to the spiritual world or using divination connections.

• Rose Pink: This is the color of love and friendship. Use it to enhance your romantic and creative skills and increase personal beauty.

- White: The classic color of divination and spirituality. This bag will help you connect to angels and improve your psychological health.

- Grey: Objects stored in grey bags will become mysterious and will be powerful when creating illusions. They will be powerful in spells involving invisibility and secretive moves.

- Black: Banishing spells and protection rituals will work better with a black mojo bag. The planet Saturn is associated with this color and provides a level of discipline.

Make Your Bag

Step One

Measure and cut your fabric so it forms a rectangle roughly three times as wide as it is long. For instance, 12 inches long and 4 inches wide.

Step Two

Fold the fabric in half so that the smooth side of the fabric is facing inward. Carefully position the ends and edges and, if necessary, trim any stray strands of fabric.

Step Three

Sew the sides of the bag, leaving the last two inches unsown, so it forms a pocket. Keep the stitching small and neat and leave the top of the bag open as this will be your opening.

Step Four

Turn your bag inside out, so the smooth side of the fabric is showing, and your stitches are hidden. Fold down the unsown fabric so it forms a flap on both sides of your bag.

Step Five

Take your scissors and carefully make four small incisions along the fold you have just created.

Step Six

Take a ribbon or colored string and thread it through the slits you have just created. Make sure the cord is long enough to encompass the neck of your bag with extra for tying.

Step Seven

Charge your bag. Place crystals, stones, herbs, and other items to make your bag fit the purpose it is meant for.

Step Eight

Draw the string tight and keep your items safe within.

Now you need to choose the objects you place in your bag. What goes in is determined by your goal and what is a proven way to achieve that goal. There will always be at least one item in your bag, and often it will come with others. Traditionally there should be an odd number of things in your bag as even numbers are considered passive while odd numbers are active and dynamic. There should never be over 13; however, as a result, it will be less effective if the bag is overfilled.

Now you need to load your bag with pertinent items. Corresponding herbs, stones, and amulets can be used along with personal objects that signal your intentions.

- For protection, use lodestone, obsidian arrowheads, basil, and a protective amulet.

- For good luck, fill your bag with dried John the Conqueror root, a rabbit foot, three-leaf clover, and lucky coins.

- For wealth and success, place a lodestone alongside John the Conqueror root with tumbled tiger eye crystals and a selenite stick.

- For love, place rosehip and magnetized sand with dried petals and rose quartz heart crystals alongside a piece of paper with a love declaration in your bag.

- For lifting a hex or crossing a jinx, put dried poke root with an alligator claw, magnetized salt, and moss agate crystal in your bag.

Once loaded, it's time to bless your bag. Blow into your open bag and repeat a prayer to bless your items. Say, *"With my breath, I bless you just like the Lord blew breath into all of us and gave us life"* Draw the cord tight and make sure your bag is secure. Use magic oil to anoint your bag with five dots or sprays. Place a dot at each corner and one in the center.

Hold your bag in your hands and repeat the phrase *"I bless you and set you a purpose, (now state that purpose) and I bind you and give you the strength to be successful."*

Now fix your purpose with a magic candle. Take nine pins and a candle and write your purpose on the candle before you impale the nine pins into it. The last pin should be inserted through the wick just before you light it and state your intention again. If you are creating a mojo, you can't overstate your intentions. Every affirmation will increase the chances of success.

Now you need to name your mojo bag and make it the physical body representing your spiritual ally. True hoodoo practitioners don't see their mojo bags as an inanimate talisman. Your mojo is part of you and, because of this, should be named. Consider it from a psychological view, the name you give your bag will help you associate a personality and energy with it, and you will begin to view your bags as friends and allies.

Tips to Help You Name Your Bag

- Listen to your heart. Once you have made your bag, you will begin to hear certain names or see a sign that indicates what to call your bag. You may dream of meeting a woman called Mary and then see the name in the press a couple of times. This will help you decide what to call your bag.

- You may decide to name the bag after yourself. For instance, if your name is Peter, you can use Little Pete or Petey. Derivations of your name make the bag more personal, but you will run out of them depending on how many bags you make.

- For a more off-the-wall name, you need to pick a person who symbolizes the endeavor you want your bag to represent. For instance, if you want to attract wealth, call your bag Elon or Bezos after the tech giants. Love mojo bags should be called Romeo or Cupid to signify their connection to romance. The base idea is your bag will take on the characteristics of the person after whom it is named.

- Look to your faith. If you are of a certain faith, then biblical names will be suitable. Samson is a great name for strength, while Adam means living. Research your choices with a baby name book to discover what different names mean.

- Let the spirits guide you. Take a random book from your bookshelf and let it fall open. There will be a name there that shouts to you and tells you what to call your bag.

Once your bag is loaded, blessed, and named, it's time to make it part of your being. For the first week, your need to keep it close to your skin. Pin it inside your clothes or wear it around your neck so it can imbue your spirit and become part of your psyche. At night pin it to the base of your pillow or keep it on your nightstand. Feed it with magic oil regularly during that first week and keep it dry and clean.

How Long Does the Mojo Bag Work?

Most bags will remain powerful for a year. There are a few guidelines to follow to keep your bag working:

1) Your bag is for your eyes only. If someone else sees or touches your bag, it can "kill your hand" and render the mojo inactive.

2) Hard items should be taken out and cleaned, while soft items like herbs and petals need to be replaced when needed.

3) Feed the bag every week on the same day as it was made by using oil to regenerate its power. Use incense smoke and prayer to feed the bag whenever you need to call upon it.

4) Keep your bag dry. If it gets wet, attempt to revive its power with the Rose of Jericho plant, aka the resurrection plant.

5) There is no reason to replace your bag after a year if it's still working for you. Time and strength can differ, and different bags work better than others. Only you will know when to make a new bag and dispose of your old one.

6) When you decide to replace your bag, treat it with respect and bury it with care. This manifestation tool has been good to you, and you need to acknowledge that.

Storing Your Mojo Bags

After the first week, store your bag carefully so it will work correctly. Choose a hardwood box that is decorative and well-sealed. Place your bag inside and choose a candle to sit on the lid. Light the candle and burn it until the wax reaches the bottom of the box. This will form a sacred seal that will protect your bag until you need it.

This method should be used if you can't access your bag to feed and re-energize it regularly. For instance, if you have a jinxing bag, just in case, but you recognize the fact that you probably won't use it, you can store it in a box for a long time. Most hoodoo followers carry their positive mojo bags with them regularly, but they leave the more negative bags in storage.

Your mojo bag can be customized to suit any need. If you are looking for a new job, you can use a green bag filled with gravel root and magnetizing salt to draw well-paid employment into your life. If you are unfortunate enough to be falsely accused of a crime, then a blend of sage, galangal (aka court case root), and other herbs will help you get your case across in court. Use your mojo bag to confuse the opposition and get the judge or jury to rule in your favor.

If you prefer to buy commercial mojo bags, know the terms "double strength" or "triple strength." Ideally, this will mean the bag contains curios that are less readily available, like a human bone or a snake rib, but sometimes it just means there are more than the normal amount of items inside. Commercial bags do work, but you empower them with your essence and spirit when you make them yourself. Hoodoo is a powerful way to protect yourself, and commercial bags are less personal but can still be effective.

Chapter 6: Begin Your Conjure Work

What is Conjure Work?

An amalgam of cultural influences is involved in conjure work. The African beliefs and the Protestant base have been combined with Germanic and East European cultural influences with traditional herbal lore and knowledge that stems from the Native American community; all melded together to form Hoodoo conjure work.

It is essential to understand that conjure work is not a stand-alone practice but is merely a spiritual paradigm that lies within the more established form of folk magic that is Hoodoo. Some may call the practices listed below rootwork or spell casting but conjure work focuses more on the bastion of traditional learning.

There are two forms of conjure work based on learning and wisdom. The first stream is based on traditional practices and wisdom passed down through generations. This can be as simple as why nobody should touch your mojo bag to spiritual workings involving powders and other magical tools.

The more formal stream of conjuring involves studying intellectual streams of magic. The conjure doctors traditionally educated themselves by studying the magical arts from texts that contained spiritual and magical knowledge from all the different cultures that Hoodoo embraces. These were in the form of grimoires and other texts containing the magic of the Ancients.

The practice of conjure work has many influences and is passed from family members to their descendants. It can change and grow with every generation and develop new branches of work. What remains constant is the source of power. The natural world is filled with innate magic sources that conjure uses to influence change in people, circumstances, and fates. Conjuring involves combining these powerful ingredients to create a potent force used to manifest their desires.

Conjuring involves various implements, and we will discuss the power of candles and rootwork in later chapters. This chapter focuses on the power that can be created by combining natural elements to form powders, salves, and oils that should be readily available to Hoodoo practitioners.

When Should You Perform Your Conjuring?

Quite simply, whenever you need to. There are no hard and fast rules regarding timing or any other aspect of Hoodoo. Do them in your own time and be governed by your needs and desires. However, the power of the moon can enhance your work and give it a little oomph!

The Full Moon and Wasting

Often seen as a time of abundance, the full moon is also a final chapter of growth. As it wanes, it gets smaller and fades into darkness. If you have something or someone in your life that needs to be diminished and banished, then perform the following ritual to dispel them from your life.

Step One: Write down the name of the thing or person you want to remove from your life.

Step Two: Slice a hole into a fresh lemon and place the paper into the fruit.

Step Three: Cover the top of the paper with a piece of red pepper.

Step Four: Sew the hole with black thread.

Step Five: Pray to your favorite deity or saint to free you from the thing or person before the new moon. Mention the new moon as you don't want the negativity to return as the moon waxes.

Step Six: For the next fifteen days, repeat your prayer and watch for signs of the removal of your intention. There may be signs put in your path as the new moon begins to reappear. For instance, if you are attempting to stop smoking, then a sign or advertisement for cut-price vapes may appear. Hoodoo is telling you it recognizes what you need and is creating a path for success. You simply must become aware and take the path it shows you.

Charging Your Lucky Talisman with the Power of the Full Moon

Normally Hoodoo doesn't rely on the moon to increase the power of the ingredients it uses. They are powerful enough and only need to be cleansed with salt to recharge their energies. The moon is used to increase the spirituality of mojo bags or personal lucky charms. Letting them charge in the new moon is considered an immensely personal experience and is not for sharing with others.

The moon is used as a timepiece for conjuring. It signals when the time is right for the rituals and how to make use of its energy. Because we are human, we are affected by the moon's power, and it makes us stronger. When conjuring, the power doesn't come from the moon. It comes from us.

The Power of Powders

Every good conjuror has a stock of powerful powders to use in their work. They can be used in different forms of magic, including powering mojo bags, dressing wallets, powering love potions, casting people from your life, or attracting love. They are used to remove jinxes and bring luck, success, and wealth in different situations. Some powders are specifically mixed for job interviews or court cases, while most are more generic.

Here are just a few examples of powders all good Hoodoo conjurors need:

Aphrodite Powder

The best time to conjure is during the new moon

Ingredients

- Dried apple skins
- Pomegranate seeds
- Organic cocoa powder
- Dried mango skin
- Hibiscus petals
- Rose petals
- Hibiscus tea leaves
- Chamomile tea leaves
- Drops of passionflower essential oil

Grind all the dry ingredients together in a pestle and mortar until it's a fine powder. Add the essential oil and store it in a glass bottle.

The Wild West Powder Used to Banish or Cross

The best time to conjure is during the waning moon

Ingredients

- 3 black cloves
- Ground black pepper
- Onion powder
- Red cayenne powder
- Cumin seeds
- Fresh paprika
- Red hot chili oil

Use a small blender to mix the ingredients or grind by hand. Store in a suitable sealed container, and make sure you wash your hands when you handle this powder.

Removing the Jinx Powder

Best conjured during a waning moon

Ingredients

- Fresh mint leaves
- Dried wintergreen leaves
- Chamomile tea leaves
- Citric essential oil

Grind the ingredients together to form a paste and add to a base ingredient like cornstarch or rice flour.

Algiers Powder

Use this powder to dust the body and attract love and romance.

Best conjured during a full moon

Ingredients

- Deadnettle leaves
- Orris root
- Dried rose petals
- Vanilla essential oil

Grind and add to base flour to create dust.

Dream Powder

Use when you feel the need to have prophetic dreams and connect to the spirits as you sleep.

Best conjured during a waxing moon

Ingredients

- Licorice tea leaves
- Cinnamon powder
- Coriander seeds
- Cardamom seeds
- Ginger

Grind and add to base flour. Sprinkle onto sheets and pillowcases before sleep.

Controlling Powder

Use this powder to gain control over others. This can be in relationships or at work.

Ingredients

- Dried saltpeter
- Magnetic sand
- Myrrh
- Epsom salts

Mix the ingredients and add to base flour.

Hard Cash Powder

The best time to conjure is when the full moon occurs on Thursday, and the number 7 or 9 is part of the date.

Use his potent powder to attract wealth and money. It can be used to improve chances when gambling.

Ingredients

- Dried leaves from potentilla plant
- Chamomile tea leaves
- Cloves
- Fresh ginger
- Dried nutmeg
- A four-leaf clover
- Fresh mint
- Lavender essential oil

Grind the ingredients and store them in a glass bottle.

Cascarilla Powder

This is a simple to make powerful powder. It can be used to create a circle of protection, or it can be added to a bath to draw negativity out. Added to a floor wash, it can cleanse your house and protect your home.

The only ingredients are eggshells. Clean them and let them dry out before grinding them to a fine powder. The result is white cascarilla powder.

To make brown cascarilla powder, simply toast the eggshells in the oven until they turn brown. Then grind them until they form a fine powder.

Powders are an essential part of conjuring, as are oils. Use these recipes to make your carrier oils that can be combined with your powders or used alone to create powerful intentions.

Oils

Confusion Oil

Use this oil to make your enemies and adversaries fight each other instead of you.

Ingredients

- 1 equal part chili pepper oil
- 1 equal part patchouli oil

Add to the oil mixture

- Grains of paradise
- Blackened peppers (red, green, chili, or bell)
- Seeds from a poppy
- Mustard seeds

Adding dried vitamin E will give your oil more potency.

Conjure Oil

This all-purpose oil is used to bring more power to your conjuring work. Use it to enhance your experiences and manifest your greatest wishes.

Ingredients

- Equal parts Frankincense
- Equal parts Sandalwood
- Equal parts lotus scented oil

Mix and store in a glass bottle.

Good Luck Oil

Create a base carrier oil from jojoba oil and add the following ingredients

- 3 drops of cinnamon oil
- 20 drops of gaultheria oil

- 15 drops of essential lavender oil

If you want the oil to be more money orientated, add ginger and vetiver oil to make the intent specific to wealth.

Van Van Oil

One of the classic oils of early Hoodoo, this recipe has been passed down for generations. Some ingredients may be unobtainable, but the absence of Asian oils won't hurt the potency. This recipe is focused on the lemongrass and citronella components which you can add to create your own floral bouquet.

Ingredients

- 32 drops of citronella oil
- 16 drops lemongrass oil
- 2 drops of palmarosa oil

This is your stock oil and is a powerful base to which you can add your personal favorites. Dried herbs and essential oils will tailor your oil to suit your purpose. When using van van oil, always dilute the solution with a clean carrier oil like natural almond oil.

Other Types of Conjuring

Most practitioners recognize modern medicine and don't profess to know better than health workers and traditional doctors. They know for certain conditions, natural substances work just as well, if not better, as medical treatments.

Traditional Headache Salve

Ingredients

- 1 cup of light organic oil, sunflower, or sesame oil work great
- White sage
- Eucalyptus
- Lavender

- ½ oz pure beeswax
- Vitamin E in a liquid form
- Material for straining

All the herbs mentioned in the recipe can be fresh or dried, and the amount you add is a personal choice. Try an ounce of each and add extra if needed.

1) Now, add all the herbs to a glass casserole dish and cover with the oil.

2) Bake in an oven for 3 hours at 180 degrees.

3) Remove from the oven and let it cool for 30 minutes.

4) Use the straining cloth to remove the herbs while squeezing all the excess liquid from the cloth.

5) Put the herbal infused oil in a stainless-steel cooking pot and simmer the liquid on a low flame for 10 minutes as you add the vitamin E-liquid.

6) Add the beeswax to the oil and continue to heat until the liquid is melted and mixed.

7) Remove the cooking pot and let it rest for 5 minutes.

8) Before the mixture sets, decant it into cosmetic jars before leaving it to set.

9) Once the salve mixture has cooled and thickened, put lids on the jars.

10) Use a smudge of the salve to relieve headaches by spreading it on your temples or forehead instead of using painkillers.

Wasps Nest Conjuring

If you are lucky enough to find a dead wasp's nest in your garden, don't throw it away. Grind the nest and any accompanying dead wasps and incorporate the powder into your banishing and hex powders.

Traditionally Hoodoo believers believed wasps nests contained powerful protective powers and the teachings of Treemonisha call the phenomenon a *dirt dauber nest*. It was believed that the wasp's nest was a bringer of luck, and it kept the evil spirits away.

Mix some of your ground wasps' nest with warm water and goofer dust to form a protective mix. To create a mixture that allows you to infiltrate another person's life, a dried wasp nest is an essential ingredient. In the natural world, wasps enter a beehive by camouflaging their smell and destroy it from the inside. If this is your intention, you can use this powerful ingredient to seek retribution from within.

How to Enhance Your Conjure Work with Psalm Recitations

All forms of spiritual workers understand the power of speech. The spoken word enhances and reinforces the power of intentions. Prayers and Holy Scriptures are the most powerful forms of this type of incantation as they bring strength and reassurance to the spirit.

This is especially important in Hoodoo works as the bible is packed full of useful information that corresponds with the practice's values. It shows us how to cleanse the soul and protect the body and home from evil.

Various Important Psalms Used to Enhance Conjure Work

Psalm 51 is used to cleanse and is often used in conjunction with healing baths. It contains powerful incantations that ask for the release of iniquities and the washing away of sins. The psalm refers to original sin and the desire to seek inner truths and become purged.

The intention cast by the psalm is strongly based on being taken into the presence of the Holy Spirit and turning away from sin. Use this psalm if you feel the need to seek salvation or restore your faith and free spirit.

Psalm 64 is used for protection. Recite it when you feel under threat or want to confront your adversaries. If you need to target a person causing you harm, write down their name on a piece of brown paper, write the psalm on a white piece of paper and burn a black candle on top of the two pieces of paper.

The psalm appeals to God to protect us from evil people who use their bitter words and forked tongues to spread evil intentions. It tells of the righteous people working with God to banish all wrongdoers and make them flee from sight.

Psalm 78 mirrors Hoodoo's beliefs perfectly. It should be recited when you need to enhance your psychic abilities or charge your talisman. Pass the magic objects from one hand to another as you recite the psalm to imbue the power of your ancestors into your conjure work.

The psalm encourages us to pass on our powers and learn from those who have passed before us. It is a powerful call to believers to talk openly about their spiritual and ancient wonders.

Psalm 29 is a cleansing psalm used to protect property rather than personal items. In the psalm, images of the Lord struck the land with lightning forks describe how God cleansed the desert and stripped back the forests of Earth. Use this psalm to deep cleanse your home and strip it of all negative energy.

Psalm 65 is the gambler's psalm. If you need extra luck or are about to gamble on a project psalm, 65 is perfect for amplifying your intentions. It describes the godly actions that take place on Earth and how we are lucky to be blessed with such abundance. The psalm should be recited when creating oils and powders for luck, success, and wealth.

Most of all, your conjuring work should incorporate both streams of work. Study scientific methods alongside your ancient grimoires to create eclectic knowledge. Call upon your guardians and ancestors to assist you in your work but don't exclude modern methods and practices. Hoodoo is a perfect mix of the traditional arts and modern components.

Chapter 7: Candle Magic

Candles have been around for millenniums and were first attributed to the ancient Egyptians and some European cultures where remains of candles and their holders were found in prominent ruins. The Romans also favored the use of candles in their ceremonies, and the tradition passed to other important religions. Buddhists and other monotheistic religions used animal fat to coat reeds and form the basic concept we know today as candles.

Despite the depiction of early Hoodoo workers using candles for their working practices, the reality is that they were unavailable to early slaves, as they didn't have access to them. Candles were costly and only used in big houses, while slave quarters were lit by grease lamps or Betty lamps, as they were known, that used household fats to provide light.

Following their Emancipation, former slaves began to travel to more urban landscapes rather than staying in rural communities. Once they formed their community's outsiders recognized a way to market candles as a key part of Hoodoo rootwork and conjuring. Shops began to appear that specialized in producing candles known as "Bend over," "Easy money," and "Swift luck" to appeal to the intentions of more traditional Hoodoo roots.

A series of booklets explaining the powerful effects of candle magic was published in the 1940s and encouraged using different types of candles and how to amalgamate their use into more traditional rituals and workings already popular with Hoodoo believers.

Today candle magic appeals to beginners for much the same reasons as it did post WW2. They are an inexpensive way to start your journey. They can be found in many forms and colors and are easily accessible. Ever since Hoodoo accepted the power of candle magic, it has also explored how different magical traditions use them and adopt their beliefs. Hoodoo is always adapting and embracing new magic, and candle magic is no exception.

The Meaning of Color in Hoodoo Candle Magic

Traditionally hoodoo workers didn't believe the color of a candle was important. They mainly worked with black and white candles as they represented the good and evil aspects of life. However, as modern Hoodoo evolves, it continues to embrace other traditional beliefs and make it part of traditional conjuring and work.

Other cultures believe the color of the candle creates vibrations and spiritual connections, but that isn't the case in Hoodoo. The magic comes from the intent and not vibrations, so why would the color of a candle be important? Many Hoodoo practitioners use colored candles to remind themselves of their intent and avoid becoming distracted. Use the colors listed below to remind you why you are performing your work and refocus your efforts. Purchase long-lasting candles to allow you to perform your magic for days rather than hours, and your intent will grow over time.

Color of Candles and Their Meanings

- White candles are used for blessings and healings. They were the original candles and represented more traditional Hoodoo beliefs.

- Black candles are used to place a hex or protect individuals.

- Red candles represent blood. The liquid of life is a powerful force and so are red candles. They form the intentions regarding love and attraction and represent boldness and audacity.

- Pink candles are used to concentrate intentions on domestic affairs. They represent togetherness and respect between family members. Pink candles are used to heal a wounded spirit and regenerate positive energies in the soul.

- Orange candles are used to create doorways and remove blockages. They create a path for success and improve mental clarity and strong intentions.

- Gold candles are burned to bring wealth and fortune.

- Yellow candles signify fortune and change. They are used to create situations that can change the workers' life; this may be in relationships or practical life.

- Green candles signify material gain. They aid magic directed toward business matters and financial gain.

- Blue candles are burned for joyful magic. They signify harmony and peace and are used to bring peace to troubled households.

- Purple candles represent mastery. To cast an intention that gives you control over others, enhance your magic by burning a purple candle.

- Silver/Gray candles are helpful when casting spells for protection. They are burned to help relieve the pain and anguish connected to grief and loss.

- Brown candles are burned to ensure success regarding legal matters. This type of magic is used for court cases and reading wills.

Hoodoo Candle Terminology

Sometimes terms used within any practice don't make sense. Candle magic is no different. You will come across certain words that are important but not self-explanatory so, here's a list of words with their meanings used in candle magic:

- **Dressed Candles**: When practitioners dress candles, they use ingredients to guide the spirits to their intentions. Generally, you would choose a candle that signals your intent and then apply oil or roots to strengthen your magic. For instance, if you need to attract protection, you would choose a gray candle and apply suitable protective oil. You can use a mixture of oils to strengthen your candle by applying Fast luck oil to attract luck and protection.

  A Quick Tip: Don't overload your candle with oil, or it may set on fire! Four to five drops are sufficient to dress a standard candle, and adding extra won't make your magic stronger and can cause excessive smoke.

- **Fixed Candles:** These types of candles are like dressed candles but are prepared by other people. They have been loaded with oils and herbs following intense prayers and loaded intent. They are available commercially and are sold in containers with printed instructions for use.

- **Loaded Candles:** When a candle has been carved into or hollowed out and then filled with oils, roots, or herbs, it is called a "loaded candle." You can load your own and tailor your candle to suit your intention, or you can buy pre-prepared candles from specialist suppliers. If doing a homemade candle, remember to choose a chunky candle as tapered ones will split and crack.

- **Carved Candles:** Carving a name or symbol into a candle is used to direct magic to a specific person or thing. Carving someone's name directs the intention of your magic towards them or makes it work for them. More generic symbols represent how you want your magic to work. For instance, the carving of an eye into a candle signifies protection.

- **Rolled Candles:** Candles rolled in oil and herbs are called "rolled candles" and can look impressive. There are some dangers when using these types of candles, as the herbs will affect how the candle burns. Exterior materials will fall off and can cause fire and smoke to appear.

All candles are potential fire hazards and should always be watched. Encased candles are safer than traditional ones and are less likely to cause damage. Holders and cases are a great way to minimize the dangers and make your magic work safe.

Hoodoo Figure Candles

Just like colored candles, effigy or form candles aren't part of traditional Hoodoo works. They are a relatively new concept and aren't meant to represent human figures or spirits. They are used to remind you of your intent and help you refocus your efforts.

Novelty-shaped candles are a cause of debate among Hoodoo believers. Certain people feel they bring the practice into disrepute and are tacky and powerless. Others believe that the physical representation greatly enhances the magic rituals. Another sticking point is what the symbols represent. Some people look at a figure and see one meaning, while others will see a contradictory representation.

As a Hoodoo candle magic practitioner, the best way to decide is to look at the shaped candle and decide what it means to you.

- **Skull Candles:** These represent the mind and are used to penetrate thoughts and redirect how you want someone to act. The color of the skull is causally related to the intention you want to set, and white skulls are particularly effective for mourning and easing grief. Skulls are also used to incite lust and passion in someone you want to attract.

- **Devil or Satan Candles:** Placed in doorways and windows, these candles will help banish evil spirits and prevent them from entering the home. Red devils are associated with base emotions like lust and passion, and their presence will spice up any rituals involving sexual intent.

- **Baphomet Sabbatical Goat:** Used to coerce others in matters that aren't sexual, the goat represents power and force. Burn these candles when you wish to dominate the thoughts of others and make them do tour bidding.

- **Cat-Shaped Candles:** Traditionally associated with luck and good fortune, burn these candles when you need your luck to turn.

- **Seven Knob Candles:** A powerful candle with seven indentations, this candle is meant to burn over seven days. You can use it to wish for one thing for seven days, or you can wish for seven different things.

- **Marriage or Lovers Candle:** The image of a loving couple in an embrace is burned to enhance love and unions. There are also separated couples which show two people back-to-back. Burn these to encourage kinder divorces or separations.

- **Money Pyramid Candle:** Often decorated with an all-seeing eye, these candles represent power and wealth. The symbolic eye will help protect your possessions and home from theft and damage.

- Witch candles are burned to represent the power of magic and energy.

Multipurpose candles on the market can represent all forms of power. The image of male and female genitalia or more traditional satanic forms can be purchased, but it doesn't mean they should be!

Double action candles do exactly what their name suggests. They provide the user with the power to reverse situations and are larger than the standard candle. One half of the candle is black, and the other half is colored to fit with your intention.

Red and black candles are burned to stop someone or something from destroying your life.

White and black candles provide a powerful original combination of the original colors. Burn these to remove a bad hex or jinx that has been applied to you or your household.

Green and black candles will help reverse your financial misfortunes.

Triple action candles are made with sections in red, white, and green and represent a time when you need help for most things in your life. They will attract love, dispel negativity and evil while drawing wealth and good luck to you.

How to Read Candle Burning

Interpreting what the flame of a candle means is subjective. It can change depending on the material used in the candle and what the wick is made from. If you plan on mastering the art of candle readings, make sure you buy your candle from the same source, so the flame they provide is consistent. To become a master candle conjurer, you should make your candles to know exactly what you are getting.

Always remember that Hoodoo is guiding you to the outcome it believes you deserve. If you choose a badly made candle and receive a message that sends you down a different path, then maybe it was meant to be. Signs and interpretation will become second nature to you as your work improves, and you will learn to read them and understand the magical meaning behind them.

Candle Flames and What They Mean

There is a myriad way a candle can burn, and they all mean different things. When you burn your magic candles, make sure the flame can burn true and isn't affected by drafts and other exterior influences.

- Steady upward flame means all is going well.

- Jumping flame means that someone is desperate to contact you. The spirits are telling you something, and only you will know what. This flame isn't necessarily negative as it can mean the spirits are showing their encouragement for your work.

- Dancing flame. When the flame is flickering from side to side rhythmically, it indicates that your energies are chaotic. It tells you to take a minute and refocus. You have the power required for successful working, but it has been distracted.

- Shrinking flame means a lack of energy. If you see this sign, it means you may take longer than expected to reach your goal.

- Heightened flame has mixed messages for you. Your work will be completed faster than you thought, but it also indicates the results may be short-lived.

- Blue flames normally are seen at the base of the wick. They mean you are on the right track and are an indication your magic will succeed.

- Green flames mean wealth. This isn't always financially important; it just means that whatever you wish for will come in abundance.

- White smoke is a positive sign from the spirits and means you are working successfully.

- Black smoke is a signal you are being worked against. You need to leave the work and cast a road opener or blockage destroying spell before you recommence with this intention.

- Noises accompanying your flame are a sure sign the spirits are trying to communicate with you. Any popping, hissing, or crackling that isn't associated with the natural burning process will alert you to their presence.

How to Read the Wax When Your Candle is Burning

This type of divination is known as ceromancy and is performed by interpreting how wax runs down a free-standing candle.

Reading the wax and how it melts is a great way to determine how your workings are progressing. If your candle is properly contained and on a level surface the readings, will be more accurate. Here are some ways to interpret the wax from your candle:

- **Tears:** If the wax looks like human tears, it indicates that tears will be shed because of your work. If they stop before the candle runs out, then the grief will be short-lived and temporary.

- **Pinnacles:** If the wax runs down the candle but doesn't reach the bottom or break off, this means that someone involved in the spells is holding on to the past. They may have grievances or issues that mean they are tainted, and your workings won't succeed.

- No wax drips indicate the highest level of success. Your workings have been perfectly executed, and you are guaranteed success.

- If the candle opens like a flower and spreads wax into an uneven puddle, it is a sign your wish has been granted, but it suggests there are other paths to be taken. Your work is far from finished, and you need to concentrate on other areas of your life.

- Wax down one side means something is off-kilter. Your spell is going to be incomplete, and you may have a spiritual imbalance.

How to Read the Wax Puddles Once the Candle Has Burned

The wax should form a recognizable shape when performing certain rituals. Heart-shaped puddles for love and flat smooth puddles when performing more neutral spells are normal, but some shapes can indicate the presence of negativity.

- Claw-like wax remnants mean someone is spreading malicious rumors and gossip about you. Repeat your work until the wax burns smoothly.

- Wax puddles that look like genitalia can indicate infidelity and troubled relationships.

- Pillars that look unnatural or monster-like show the spell has been unsuccessful due to outside turbulence. Cast powder or oil to remove these influences.

- Coffin-shaped puddles mean that your hex or jinx spells worked, and the threat against you is defeated.

Chapter 8: The Craft of Rootwork

During the era of slavery, control was stripped from slaves' lives. They had little or no control over how they lived. While their masters may have retained control of their bodies, they had no say in how the slaves retained their spirits. Their imagination and the gift of stories meant they could keep their spirits up even during the most harrowing times.

There are multiple stories about men from Africa called John or Jack who inspired the slaves with stories of their deeds and how they got one over on their masters. Perhaps the most famous is High John, the conqueror and a huge man who hated being a slave. His trickery and skill at avoiding work made him one of the most celebrated figures in African folklore.

High John the Conqueror

Some say that High John was an African prince sold into slavery, while other tales tell of a commoner. His trickery and ability to avoid work were legendary. His strength and luck ensured that every bet he laid was successful, and although he played dumb, he always outsmarted those who opposed him. He was associated with the

Ipomea Jalapa, known as the most powerful root in a Hoodoo worker's bag of tricks.

Most practitioners always carry High John Root with them to remove obstacles and conquer their enemies. It magnifies the root's lucky element when it's stored in a green mojo bag, and it will help attract money and wealth to the carrier. Use the chips from the root to enhance cooking and use them in oils to dress your salads.

Other Popular Roots and Herbs Used in Hoodoo and Their Magical Properties

Angelica Root

Also known as Archangel root, sprinkle dried angelica in the four corners of your home to protect it and ward off evil. Use the root to enhance any workings aimed at purification and uncrossing hexes. Angelica will also help bring back lost loves and reignite passions.

Bats Head Root

Also known as Devil pod, horny bulls head, and ling nut, this strange-looking black root appears just like the head of a devil. Use it when you want your wishes to come true and remove those that stand in your way.

Blood Rot Root

Use this root for multiple results. It helps resolve marital and family disputes while improving your sex life. Burning the root during a ritual will stop someone else from taking your lover, while placing it in the window will attract new partners. Blood rot root is a popular ingredient for marriage-based rootwork.

Calamus Root

This root should be burned while performing other works to strengthen the potency of the original spell. It is a dominating root and adds strength to any situation.

Devils Shoestring Root

Use this to change your luck at work or attract a new job. Carry it in your pocket when seeking employment or attending interviews. This root will also help you gain control over the opposite sex.

Fennel

Hang fennel in your home and workplace to protect you from negative energies and spirits. It is especially effective for women and can attract money and wealth for females.

Hazel

It is used to make amulets for fertility that are traditionally given to new brides as a gift. Hang hazel twigs from windows to ward off lightning strikes.

Lavender

This herb is used to bring harmony and mutual sexual satisfaction to couples experiencing problems in the bedroom. Some Hoodoo rootworkers use it to stop cruel partners from abusing their spouses by rubbing it on the victim as a shield.

Magnolia

Males use buds from this herbal flower to attract female attention. It is also used to elicit fidelity and stop partners from straying.

Nutmeg

This lucky herb is a favorite for gamblers. It attracts wealth and luck, so it is regarded as a sign of prosperity.

Galangal Root

Known as Chewing John root, this is a powerful protection root. Chew it in your mouth while casting reverse hex spells and then spit the remains out to dispel them from your life. If you face a court case, burn this root two weeks before the court date for guaranteed success. When used to attract wealth, wrap money around the root, and it will multiply threefold.

Ginger

Most people who know about healthy eating know the benefits of ginger. Hoodoo is no different, and ginger is one of the most versatile roots used in rootwork. It is used to promote sensuality, self-confidence, and prosperity. Use it to speed up your rootwork and add an extra dose of potency. If you can source a ginger root that resembles the human form, you can perform powerful magic, and cast commanding spells with ease.

Queen Elizabeth Root

Also known as orris root, this is especially influential when used in rootwork and conjuring for love and sex. It attracts the opposite sex while increasing the potential for long time love. It is used in spells to strengthen marriage and increase fertility. Sprinkle it on sheets for some passionate nights filled with love and great sex.

Hyssop

This cleansing herb is sourced from Southern Europe and is part of the mint family. Its benefits have been known to herbal practitioners as far back as Biblical times. In Hoodoo, it is a forceful herb when used to cleanse the home and remove hexes.

Five Finger Grass

Also known as cinquefoil, this herb is used to attract success. Bathe in water infused with five-finger grass solution for nine days to remove a stubborn curse or jinx. You can make tea with dried leaves that improve your health and wealth when drunk.

Licorice Root

Use when you need to change someone's mind or gain control of their thinking. Licorice is a powerful ingredient when used in controlling powders.

Mugwort

Also known as Artemisia vulgaris, use a solution containing this herb to clean your magical tools like crystals and talismans. It will remove negativity and restore their strength. Place it in your shoes before you go out for extra energy and a spring in your step!

Parsley

These tasty leaves are much more than a handy cooking ingredient. They are used to promote calm and peace in the household and can guard your food against any form of contamination. Parsley is used for aiding healing following serious illness or surgery and is used in spells about health and vitality. If you feel out of sorts or stuck in a rut, cast a conjure using parsley, and you will immediately feel the benefits.

Pepper Tree

It stands as a powerful form of protection, and it also has healing properties and can aid the recovery of people who have been ill or had surgery.

Thyme

If you need to boost your psychic powers or purify your rootwork, thyme will help you gain knowledge and courage to carry on. It is commonly used for grounding spells and conjuring.

Witch Hazel Bark

Here we see one of the influences that Native Americans brought to Hoodoo practitioners. It is used to heal skin conditions and can be used as a gargle to treat oral problems. When incorporated into rootwork, it reduces passion and encourages chastity in those who may need to focus on other subjects. Carrying it on your person also helps reduce grief following a death.

This list is far from comprehensive, and there are thousands more herbs and roots available. They all have slightly different properties, and you can explore them ad infinitum. Hoodoo is primarily about discovering new ways to encompass other beliefs and cultures into your personal magic, and studying how other religions and beliefs use nature is one way to expand your knowledge.

How to Create Amulets and Talismans with Your Roots and Herbs

First, let's distinguish the two terms and what the difference is between them. An amulet is a natural object that can be blessed and consecrated for use in magic and conjuring. Amulets are then charged with intention depending on the power the user requires. They can be charged with attractions and with repelling powers to keep the wearer safe and lucky.

Talismans are man-made objects charged similarly. They can be crafted from many materials and worn around the neck, as a ring, or any other way the user requires. They can be decorated with natural objects like crystals or stones, but they are made by hand, often by the rootworker who is going to charge them.

How to Make an Amulet

Choose a durable material to create your amulets, like stone or gemstones. For this example, we will use a stone known in spiritual circles as a Hag stone. This is a stone that has been naturally worn down by running water to create a hole or holes that are ascetically pleasing.

The shape of your stone may immediately suggest to you what its potential power may be. A heart-shaped rock will be ideal for love spells and rootwork, while a stone that resembles a dagger will be used for protection. Now you need to make your amulet wearable. Use cords and natural fibers to enable the wearer to use it as a necklace or bracelet.

Now your talisman needs to be consecrated and cleansed. Use water and sacred salt to remove any impurities and negativity from your amulet and let it dry naturally. Now pass the stone through the burning smoke of your preferred herbs until you feel it is ready to be charged.

Charging your amulet is a personal experience and involves you calling to your favorite deities and asking them to hear your intentions. Ask them to protect you and your amulet in times of danger and bestow their love and strength on you when you need them.

Although the talisman is a natural object, that doesn't mean you can't decorate it. Use magical symbols and vibrant paint to make your amulet decorative and increase its magical potency. Add beads and crystals to the cords you used and make your amulet a stunning piece of jewelry.

How to Make a Talisman

Choose the central object you want to be the focus of your talisman. This can be a pendant you already use or a ring. You can use coins and other metal objects like keys or decorative wirework to make your piece look beautiful. Clay and metal objects can be engraved with special symbols or sigils that can be incredibly powerful in the use of your talismans.

Determine what the purpose of your talisman is. Do you need it to attract love, or is it a more protective charm? You can use the lunar cycles to enhance your talisman's strength by choosing the best time of the month to create your piece. Use leather straps to make your talisman wearable, as leather represents an amalgam of the natural and man-made world.

Use your herbs and roots to create a potion or infusion to bless your talisman. Sprinkle it with a few drops daily, and make sure you keep your talisman in a safe place. Now charge your talisman with your inner energy. Allow the strength of your intentions to wash over the piece until it vibrates with your spirit. Summon your favorite spirits and deities and ask for their blessing and protection in all your works.

If you have any excess energy in your physical body, cast a simple grounding spell like the one below:

Burn sage and sandalwood on a slate disc and light a white candle that sits on top of a natural stone. Seat yourself in a comfortable position and connect to the flame your candle is creating. Stare at it as it dances and breathe deeply as you watch.

Now visualize roots growing from your arms and legs. Imagine them burrowing into the ground and revel in your connection with the earth and the universe. Now use these roots to channel all the anxieties and fears you have ever felt and feel them disappear into the ground. Focus on your breath as you feel your excess energies and negativity drain away.

Grounding yourself is not just about getting rid of anxiety and feeling chilled. It is all part of your spiritual connection to the very fabric of the cosmos and the power it holds. Let the candle burn for an hour after you have completed the grounding, so it infuses into every fiber of your being. Once the candle has burned down, the stone it was sitting on can be used as a natural amulet.

Although there are no hard and fast rules regarding the use of these objects, most people find that talismans are more effective for attraction and projections, while amulets are used for protection and repelling.

How to Use Magic Herbs and Roots in Your Spell Work

1) Rolling your candles in dried herbs and roots will help your candle burn more effectively.

2) Burn dried herbs or roots on charcoal or slate disks

3) Use as incense

4) Sturdy herbs can be burned directly. Flammable herbs include sage, rosemary, eucalyptus, and Italian cypress, but you must always take precautions

5) Use them to make tinctures so their power will continue to work for months at a time.

How to Prepare and Harvest Your Roots

Fall is the perfect time to begin your harvesting. All the vibrant energy of summer has retreated into the plants' roots that bloomed, and the goodness and nutrients are firmly ensconced within. This makes it the perfect time to harvest and prepare roots for use.

You need to respect the plants you harvest and make sure you cause no damage. Ask the plants for permission to use their bounty before you carefully take what you need.

Here is a timeframe to help you become a sustainable herb and root master

• Annual plants should be harvested once their full cycle has been completed

• Perennials shouldn't be harvested in the first three years because the active compounds they contain won't be present until they have matured

- More substantial shrubs and bushes will have prolific offshoots that allow you to harvest without disturbing the main taproot. This helps their chances of survival and growth

- The sap is affected by solar cycles, so harvest your roots in the morning or early evening when the vitality and energy is at premium levels

Cleaning Your Roots

Remove the soil and dirt gently and with care. An old toothbrush is perfect as it can remove the dirt without removing the tiny hairs that cover the roots. These hairs are packed with important constituents that need to be preserved.

Any cutting needs to be done when fresh as dry roots are difficult to cut cleanly. Once you have cut your roots to the required size, you need to dry them sympathetically. This can be done by laying the cuttings on trays, placing them outside out of direct sunlight but in a warm atmosphere. You can use a food dehydrator on a low setting of 150 degrees or a regular oven on a low setting with the door left open.

Quick Note: Some roots will attract moisture and become soft, discard any limp or flaccid roots immediately.

There are different rituals for charging your herbs and roots and preparing them for rootwork, so here is a general tutorial you can adapt for your uses

- Place your herbs and roots on a sacred surface and bless them with a prayer or psalm

- Use a smudging stick to bless the offerings

- Leave the roots and herbs outside in the light of the full moon

- Place the roots and herbs in a container filled with sacred salt

Chapter 9: The Hoodoo Divination

In the past, divination rituals were often reserved for professional sightseers and who had the gift of fortune-telling. Ordinary people would seek their help and ask them to do readings on their behalf. As the practice of Hoodoo grew, our hardworking ancestors realized that they could perform rituals, but they didn't have the means to purchase fancy accessories like tarot cards and crystals to carry out their rituals.

Household objects and other tools they had to hand were substituted for their divination rites. Ordinary cards were used instead of tarot cards, and commonly sourced objects replaced ivory in the practice of cleromancy.

Here we study how modern-day Hoodoo followers can gain an insight into what the future holds for them and others.

Cartomancy

When you play a poker game or other household games, most people don't realize they are playing with the tarot card's original form. As far back as the 14th-century, gypsies used ordinary cards to foresee the future. The four suit designs were designed to represent the four elements of earth, wind, fire, and water. Each suit then contains a hierarchy that represents the leaders and their subjects. The King and queen are served by their pages, and the rest of the cards represent the subjects who serve them. The 52 cards all have separate meanings that govern how you read a spread.

Card Spreads

This is the term used to describe how the cards are dealt and what to expect from certain combinations.

- Single cards are used for rapid answers to straightforward questions

- Three-card spreads are used to signify the past, present, and future

- Nine-card spreads are used to represent the past, present, and future with added layers of information

- The Gypsy Spider Web is a tableau of cards made up of 21 individual cards in three rows of seven to create a detailed reading of the past, present, and future.

There are myriad ways of creating card spreads and possible interpretations. The hidden nuances behind the spread will mean different things to different people. However, a basic knowledge of what the cards represent will help you get an accurate and informative reading.

The Definition and Meanings Behind the Cards

The Suits

- **Hearts:** Representing the element of fire, this suit is connected to the home and emotional affairs

- **Diamonds:** Representing the element of wind, this suit is connected to work-related affairs and other external issues

- **Clubs**: Representing the element of earth, and this suit relates to financial and money related matters

- **Spades**: Representing the element of water, and this suit is related to obstacles and roadblocks that can cause problems in your life

The Individual Cards and Their Meaning

Hearts

The regal cards of the pack are known as identifier cards and will represent a certain person in your life

- **King**: A sage man who will give excellent advice
- **Queen**: A kindly lady with light hair
- **Jack**: A younger person of indistinctive gender with blonde hair
- **Ten:** Joy and happiness
- **Nine:** Your wishes and hopes will all come true
- **Eight:** your social life will improve as you get invited to parties
- **Seven:** Broken promises and treachery
- **Six**: Serendipity and good fortune
- **Five**: Envious people surround you
- **Four**: A change of surroundings and maybe marriage later in life
- **Three:** Slow down and be cautious
- **Two:** Solidifying a relationship with engagement, success, and wealth
- **Ace:** New beginnings, love, and joy

Diamonds

- **King:** Powerful, stubborn, and obstinate man with light hair

- **Queen:** Flirtatious woman fond of partying and loves to chat about others

- **Jack:** A younger person with light hair. The black sheep of the family with a dubious past

- **Ten:** New environment. Positive changes and success

- **Nine:** Unexpected financial news, new career opportunities, change

- **Eight:** Marriage in maturity, traveling in cold environments, money changes

- **Seven:** Unexpected gifts, work-related issues

- **Six:** Issues with second marriages

- **Five:** Career success, happy family life

- **Four:** Unexpected legacies or bequests, money

- **Three:** Issues with legal matters, family disputes

- **Two:** Love affairs that aren't conventional and aren't popular, fallouts between business partners

- **Ace:** Gifts of jewelry, correspondence regarding financial matters

Clubs

- **King:** Loving man with dark hair who is magnanimous and kind

- **Queen:** Older woman with dark hair who is attractive and confident

- **Jack:** Younger friend with dark locks who is constant and reliable

- **Ten:** Surprising financial news, foreign travel, luck

- **Nine:** New romantic relationships, be more accepting and indulgent

- **Eight:** Marriage and relationship issues, others envy you

- **Seven:** Beware the opposite gender, wealth, and success

- **Six:** Seek help with money matters; you will succeed in business matters

- **Five:** New acquaintances and a happy marriage, friends who will come to your assistance

- **Four:** Bad times lie ahead, and you will encounter betrayal and dishonesty

- **Three:** Marriage to a wealthy partner, financial assistance from your spouse

- **Two:** backstabbing and lies will disappoint you

- **Ace:** Your post will contain a letter about finances, happiness, health, and wisdom

Spades

- **King:** A powerful man who is self-confident and has jet black hair

- **Queen:** A dark-haired widow who is immoral and deceitful

- **Jack:** A younger man with questionable ethics but is well-meaning and immature, dark-haired males

- **Ten:** Incarceration, bad news, bad luck, and worries

- **Nine:** Low energy, general misfortune, death and destruction, overall depression

- **Eight:** Disrupted plans, cancellations, and disputes at work and home

- **Seven:** Lost companions, friendships destroyed, possible losses

- **Six:** Small triumphs that add up to major changes

- **Five:** Outside influences will disrupt your family life; expect a reversal of fortunes

- **Four:** Times of bad health, broken pledges, financial worries

- **Three**: Infidelity and breakdown of relationships

- **Two**: Difficult decisions regarding marriage and partnership, separation and lies

- **Ace**: Death and disruption, arguments, and obsessions

Of course, some people play their card games with jokers, and cartomancy is no different. If you see a joker in your spread, it means new beginnings and taking risks.

How to Shuffle the Deck

Everyone has their own style of shuffling and cutting the deck. If someone shuffles for a short time, this means they are more likely to want an answer for specific questions right away. Those who shuffle more are interested in a broader spectrum style of reading.

Readers should ask seekers to cut the deck into multiple piles before creating the required spread. Seekers who cut shallow are reluctant to trust the advice they will be given, while a deep cut indicates confidence and belief in the reader. Shallow cutters also worry about just how much of their true nature is about to be relieved and are anxious about the reading.

Truly gifted cartomancy readers rely on a mix of knowledge of what the cards mean and their own intuition. The spread is just the start of a journey into self-discovery for both the reader and the seeker, and the more you practice, the better your results will be.

Augury

This form of divination involves reading omens and signs to foretell the future. Hoodoo is firmly rooted in the natural world, so it follows that omens and signs that occur in nature are a trusted indication of the future. The practice was recorded as far back as Ancient Egyptian times, yet the use of formal augury is thought to be Roman.

The word auspice is derived from the Latin terms *auspicium* and *auspex*, which means "looking at birds," so the original practitioners based their beliefs on birds' movement and the patterns they formed.

If you would like to learn how to perform this particular form of divination, you can seek wild birds to read. However, the most powerful first step you can take is to let the birds come to you. You can practice the art of divination in the wild, but the most significant messages will come from birds who visit you. It is a message from the divine world, after all!

What Different Types of Birds Mean

Crows and Ravens

Black birds are often connected to bad luck and death. Maybe because they are black and have strong associations with witchcraft, or maybe because black is the color of evil. Either way, modern misconceptions should be ignored when practicing augury. These birds are the harbinger of benevolent messages, and they bring protection and good luck. Crows and ravens are two of the smartest animals in the world and, as such, should be linked to positive connections with the spiritual plane.

Hawks

These types of birds represent foresightedness and the need to take notice of your surroundings. Their superior eyesight in the wild signifies your need to see things clearly and view the bigger picture with wisdom and careful consideration. Seeing a hawk should be considered a blessing.

Owls

In some cultures, owls are psychopomps. This is a creature or spirit sent to earth to guide a soul to heaven following their death. Because of these beliefs, Hoodoo augury regards the appearance of an owl as a sign someone will die. Native Americans believe evil spirits send the owl to spy on humans and perform negative tasks on Earth.

Hummingbirds

These beautiful, strong, and fast birds are a joy to behold. Their appearance means the spirits are sending you a message of joy and love. The dance they perform is nature's way of displaying what perfect balance and harmony look like and how we must strive to achieve it in our own lives.

Doves

These white birds are often seen as a sign of hope and good intentions, while others see them as symbols of death and grief. Just like all black birds aren't negative signs, all-white birds aren't positive signs.

How Many Birds Are There?

Now consider the number of birds interacting with each other. Are there two? Are there ten? Or are there too many to count? Here an understanding of numerology will help you, but it isn't essential. If you see solo birds, they are a message to individuals to recharge and refuel their psychic and physical batteries. Pairs of birds signify romance or joining, while multiple birds show the strength of belief. Augury is all about how you interpret these signs, so you may see a recurrence of your favorite number if the spirits are trying to connect.

How Are the Birds Behaving?

The bird's physical behavior is a crucial part of the process. Are they just flying, or are they behaving differently? When you study the way birds behave, you will soon pick up on any anomalies. When a storm is coming, birds will act out of character so they could be warning you of physical dangers. Are they looking for food or a mate? This could mean you are being told to get yourself out there and improve your social ties.

How to Read Birds Flight Patterns

The position of the birds is also important. Are they concentrated in the East, or are they flying south? The ancient teachings tell us that the four directions of the compass are important when reading bird augur. The cardinal directions can mean different things.

- South represents love, heat, and passion and indicates you need to pay attention to these areas

- East indicates the Garden of Eden. It signifies a place of safety and salvation where you can find security and love

- West has two differing associations. Because the sun sets in the West, it is considered a place of darkness and cold. However, because of its association with the biblical figure Abraham, it also signifies a divine blessing and liberation from your enemies.

- North can mean permanence, or it can be read as a sign of destruction depending on your biblical leanings.

Just as these cardinal points have mixed messages, so do other aspects of augury. Dead birds would seem to represent death, but they can just mean a metaphorical death like the end of a relationship. The main point to remember is to have fun with your augury and take from it the knowledge you need and the comfort you seek.

Cleromancy

The ancient art of bone reading may seem at odds with the modern world with its use of bones as fortune-telling tools. The truth is you can use all kinds of cool stuff to perform cleromancy like dominos, stones, shells, or dice to cast your bones.

If you prefer traditional methods, then poultry bones leftover from a chicken dinner are perfect for making your tools.

How to Cure Bones

Boil some water in a large pot or your favorite cauldron and keep it on the flame. Now put your leftover bones in the pot and boil them for 20 minutes.

Once all the flesh has been stripped off, take them from the pot and let them cool down. Fill a plastic container or bucket with a mixture of ½ gallon of water plus ¼ cup of bleach. Soak the bones for an hour.

Once the bones are clean, place them in the sunlight to dry for at least a day.

Bless your bones with some sage smudging or place them in sacred salt while sprinkling anointed oil on them. Ask for divine help and appeal to your favorite deities as you work.

How to Use Your Bones

The Yes/No Method

Take a bone and ask a question. Now drop it from your hand onto your table or altar. If the bone lies in a vertical position, the answer is no, and if it's horizontal, the answer is yes.

Scrying

This is a more exacting science. Like reading tea leaves, scrying involves reading the pictorial message the bones are displaying. Take your bones and drop them onto a table or altar from a height of 12". Now consider what the bones are telling you. Just concentrate and let your mind be filled with images and ideas that appear.

The Drawstring Bag Method

Personalize your bones with images. Letters or symbols representing your creativity and energy can be combined with keywords or drawings to make your readings more intense. Ask your question as you draw bones out of a drawstring bag and apply the meanings to your dilemmas.

This type of divination is also known as sortilege. Any objects can be included in your personalized divination set, so create a sortilege kit with more personal items and fewer occult pieces. These can include feathers, pieces of driftwood, buttons, pieces of jewelry, and decorative rocks.

Most diviners will tell you that the best way to get accurate readings is to create your own set. Include unique and powerful pieces that resonate with your life. These can include commercially available items, but you shouldn't buy completed sets if you want your readings to be specific to you.

Oneiromancy

The art of divination through dreams is possibly the simplest form of connecting with the spiritual plane and the Divine. You need only to sleep and await the messages they send. They will have different meanings depending on the recipient, but some common interpretations of dream images shown below will help you decide what your dreams are telling you.

Most Common Dreams and What They Mean

1) **Teeth Falling Out:** Often interpreted as a signal of death, more symbolically, it represents a loss of vitality. The spirits are telling you to take care of yourself and increase your energy levels.

2) **Driving:** Vehicles represent our soul, and when you dream of driving, it represents the evolution of your life. If you dream you are a passenger, it could signify you need to take charge of your own decisions.

3) **Flying:** You are ready to make changes and advance your life. You are headed for a time of decisions and new beginnings.

4) Spiders: The fear and anxiety caused by arachnids represent an authoritative figure causing you stress. This could be an overwhelming relationship issue or a work problem.

5) Climbing a Mountain: This dream represents an inner need for knowledge. You are striving for self-improvement and advancement. The spirits are telling you to believe in yourself and climb the spiritual mountain that leads to your elevation.

Some Hoodoo rituals can prepare you for clearer dreams and signify you are ready to receive your messages from the spirits. Use candles, incense, and herbal tea to create a calming atmosphere before you go to sleep. Leave offerings to the deities and spirits on your nightstand to encourage them to communicate via dreams.

The moon and other elements will help you enhance the rituals and make them successful. Morpheus is the ultimate god of sleep and dreams, but you can call upon any deity you like. Hypnos, Diana, Chandra, and Ira are all symbolic figures from different cultures.

Chapter 10: Hoodoo Spells for Love and Attraction

As the song tells us, "Love is all you need," and most of us hope and pray that our romantic relationships and attachments are successful and happy. In the real world, we know that love and passion are often the catalysts for some of the most destructive emotions and actions we will be subject to. Love binds us to people, and even when threatened, we will fight for our love and resort to all methods to keep it in our lives.

Our relationships are often the basis of how we live, and most couples know they need work. Wise pairings will work together to resolve issues and treat each other with respect. Outside influences will always affect relationships with families interfering and other parties trying to create problems. Jealousy and losing trust are often the key factors that cause strife and difficulties, even for the most loved couples.

Love spells may seem like the perfect way to strengthen bonds and restore the affection and love that may have been lost. Casting spells and conjures offers solutions to problems and can seem like the last alternative for failing relationships.

The truth is that if a relationship is failing, it may be for the right reasons, and no amount of Hoodoo or other interference will save it. One person may be ready to quit and leave to look for love elsewhere, while another may feel like the love is worth saving. In situations like this, then no spell or potion will work to keep them together. You can only influence and strengthen true emotions, and if the attraction isn't there, then the spell won't work.

How to Cast Spells for You and Your Partner

If you are experiencing difficulties, but you still feel you can save your relationship, then a soul mate spell will help you come together again. Have a full and frank discussion where you both air your views before you undertake any Hoodoo rituals so you can both benefit from the power of the magic.

Create a Safe Space

Ensure that both of you are in a good space, mentally and physically. If you are surrounded by positive energy, you will be more receptive to the spell and less likely to suffer any harm.

Now create a safe space to cast your spell. Form a circle of protection using herbs, sacred salt, and crystals and enter it when you feel ready. Breathe deeply and use prayers and recitations to make your space feel special.

There are several deities associated with love and passion; you can choose your favorite from the following:

- Aphrodite, the Greek goddess of love
- Cernunnos, the Celtic horned god of passion
- Dionysus, the Greek god of fertility, winemaking, insanity, and madness
- Ishtar, the Mesopotamian goddess of sexual love
- Ptah, the Egyptian goddess of fertility and love
- Odin, the Norse god of fertility and strength

- Krishna, the Hindu god of compassion, tenderness, and love

Choose your spell carefully and be aware it comes with consequences. Do your research and consult with expert practitioners to choose the spell you need. Follow the instructions carefully and establish what the different outcomes will be. White magic is a more successful path to choose when casting romance spells, but sometimes the darker magic works better when banishing lovers or getting rid of your competition.

Examples of Available Spells and How to Perform Them

Quick Conciliation Spell

This is used to bring partners back together following an argument or separation period because of a disagreement.

What You Need

- Handwritten psalm 32
- Pink tapered candle
- 8 tacks
- Jar of honey
- Apiece of slate to burn the candle on
- Pin or needle

Take the paper you have written the psalm on and turn it over. Now write the name of the person you argued with on the paper.

Take the pin or needle and carve the name of your loved one into the candle three times.

Stand the candle on the piece of slate and surround the base with the tacks.

Cover the tacks with spoons of honey to sweeten the pain caused by your argument.

Burn the candle for three consecutive days while reciting Psalm 32. After the third day, your spell is cast.

Honey Jar Spell

If you feel your relationship has become staid or boring and you want to restore the love and romance (not the lust, that's a whole different spell!) to your life, then try this spell.

What You Need

- Pen and paper
- Slate to place your candle on
- Pink or red candles
- Your preferred love herbs and roots like cloves, rose petals, cardamom, and magnolia
- Attraction oil or powder
- Jar with honey in it

Honey is often used to attract other people because that is its natural state. Bees are drawn to honey and nectar, and so it will attract love. In ancient days honey was also used as offerings to love and fertility deities to access their gifts.

Take the piece of paper and write the name of the person you want to reconnect to three times. Now rotate the paper and write your name three times, so it overlaps their name and forms a block. Circle the block with loving words and phrases like "love me" and "come back to me" without lifting your pen from the paper.

Now add the oils and herbs to the paper. You can add some personal items to strengthen your honey and infuse it with your intentions. Use hair from your heads or even bodily fluids (use your imagination here) to enhance the mix. All these items should be kept in the center of the paper.

Now charge the jar with herbs, roots, and other items related to loving. Rosemary represents fidelity, while orange peel signifies joy. Use your favorite ingredients to charge the honey before you add the paper.

Now place the paper into the honey jar while reciting the following words *"This honey is sweet to me just like (say the name of the person you are influencing) will be sweet and loving to me."*

Lick any excess honey from your hands and repeat the ritual a further two times. Close the lid of the jar and place it in a cool place. Your honey jar of love is now complete and ready for use.

Place your candle on the slate and use the honey from the jar to anoint it. Light the candle and ask for help from the spirits and deities of love. Repeat for three days, and the spell will be cast.

Dragons Blood Resin Love Spell

While the name sounds quite dark, this spell is performed using natural ingredients to make your former lover aware that you still love them and compel them to return. It will work to make them return and give your relationship another chance at working.

What You Need

- Embers for burning

- Copper dish

- Dragon's blood resin or essential oil (Dragon's blood is a natural product obtained from tropical plants and sold by specialist Hoodoo stores)

Perform this ritual when the moon is turning from new to full. Whenever possible, this should be on Friday at midnight. Take the embers from a fire and place them in the copper bowl. Sprinkle your oil or resin over the embers and recite the following incantation:

"This dragon's blood is mine to burn just as my lovers' heart is mine to turn. May they have no pleasure or rest until they return to my loving arms. This is how it should be, and so it will be"

The spell is now cast.

How to Get Rid of an Unwanted Lover

This spell is effective when you want to get rid of your lover or break up a couple who shouldn't be together.

What You Need

- Red rose
- Paper with the names of your lover or the couple written on it by you
- 4 nails
- Hammer

Take the paper and dress it with banishing oils or herbs. Garlic, pepper, and sage all work effectively. Fold the paper so it can be enfolded into the petals of the rose. Now find a dead tree and nail your rose/paper combination to it with the four nails. Now beat the flower until it is destroyed. Walk home without casting a backward glance, and your spell is cast.

A White Candle Spell to Attract New Love

This spell is meant for both sexes and is designed to attract love and tenderness. This will not be in the form of a thrall or zombie-like passion, but it will attract all the love that person has for you. This natural form of love is more likely to lead to a successful relationship as it comes from the heart. Accept the level of love you will receive and work on developing your true connections.

What You Need

- An altar or decorated table
- White marriage candle (a plain white 4" altar candle will also work)
- Thorn from a white rose bush

First, decorate your altar or table with objects that symbolize yourself and the object of your love. These can be keepsakes, items of clothing, pictures, and mementos of your time together.

Now take the thorn and inscribe the candle with the phrase *"Come to me, my love"* and the name of the person you want to attract. Repeat until the phrase and the name have been written three times. Burn the candle upon your altar ad visualize your lover coming toward you with loving intentions, completely naked and filled with beauty.

Once the candle has burned down, collect the wax puddle and the other objects from your altar and store them in a safe place. Make sure you know exactly where they are because if you wish to cast off this person in the future, you will need to dispose of the items ceremoniously. Cast the objects and the wax into a fire or bury them at a crossroads to reverse the spell and dispose of any love from this person.

Passion and Lust Spells

Love is great, but sometimes you need to feel baser instincts like lust and passion. These following spells will help you get the oomph back in the bedroom. These spells are great for couples who need some help or can be used to ignite a spark in someone you know but don't have a relationship with.

Casting your spells as the moon is waxing at nine o clock in the evening will make your spell more potent. Performing the spell when the moon is in the house of Taurus will also help your spells' success.

Passion Spell

What You Need

- A clean sterilized pin or needle
- An apple
- Patchouli incense stick

If you perform this spell as a couple, you must both prick your fingers to release a drop of blood. Let the two drops fall on the incense before you light it. If you perform the ritual alone, use two drops of your own blood to symbolize the union.

Light the incense and pass the apple through the smoke three times. Each time you pass, say these words, *"Blood of (your name) mix with the blood of (your partners' name) and become united as one."*

Now slice the apple in half and lay it before the incense stick. The spell is now cast, so prepare yourself for some lustful times ahead!

Easy Lust Spell

This spell is designed to explode euphoric lust between partners that have lost the spark they once had. Use the spell to induce sexual feelings that may have become dormant.

What You Need

- A pink altar candle
- Clean pin
- Rosewater
- Organic honey

This spell will provoke lust in someone to whom you are not romantically attached but who is aware of your presence. Use the pin to etch the name of your potential lover nine times on the candle. Mix the rosewater with a drop of honey and anoint the candle. Don't use too much honey, or the candle will turn into a torch.

Light the candle for nine minutes every night for nine nights.

Once the ritual has finished, wrap the candle's remnants in a piece of red silk and bury it at the foot of a fruit-bearing tree. Your spell is now cast.

These types of spells are some of the most popular magic. Most couples have periods when their relationship is less than perfect, and they need some help. Keeping passion and lust alive when raising a family or working can be difficult. Spells won't fix broken relationships, but they can improve certain areas. Don't try and force people to stay when they know it's time to leave.

Let the negative thoughts you have go before casting your spells. Trust that your magic will work, and the outcome will be the one you hope for. There is always hope and positivity attached to this kind of magic, and you should celebrate this fact. If you have lost confidence in your partnership, then casting a love spell will help you remember why you first loved each other.

Using spells to attract people is a powerful tool, but it needs to be used realistically. Don't try and attract people who are outside of your social circle. Some deluded people try casting spells to attract celebrities and famous people. This won't work. You need to limit your expectations and choose realistic goals.

Chapter 11: Hoodoo Spells for Luck and Wealth

Now we switch the focus from matters of the heart to matters of the pocket. Luck and wealth are always welcome in our lives, and some people believe that luck attracts much more than financial wealth. Lucky people seem to have the best lives. Their friends are great, they have the best jobs and live in the best places. Luck is more than just succeeding in gambling terms. Being lucky means that things just go your way, so why wouldn't we want to attract luck into our lives?

Before you perform these Hoodoo rituals, it is doubly important to create the right space for your work. Luck and wealth will come to you wherever you perform your spells, but if you take the time to set the scene, your spells will be more powerful and bring greater rewards.

Set Up an Altar Designed to Attract Luck and Wealth

This isn't as complicated as it sounds! An altar need not be a complex wooden structure with ornate carvings or a religious tone. Your altar could be as simple as the top of a small cabinet or a table set up in your home. The main thing to remember is an altar should be used only for spells and magic work. You shouldn't use a piece of furniture used daily for other purposes.

Make your altar personal and representative of your beliefs. You can use different colored candles and coverings to indicate your intentions as you perform different types of magic.

When practicing spells to attract luck and wealth, you need to utilize the strength of the color green. Cover your altar with a green cloth and use green colored candles to decorate it.

Charge your space with the four elements by placing a jar of sand to the north, a bowl of water to the west, your green candle to the south, and an incense stick to the east. This represents the power of earth, water, fire, and air.

You can charge your altar with representations of lucky gods and goddesses to improve your work; here are some of the most popular deities:

- Ganesh, the Indian god who represents prosperity and attainment
- Mahakala, the Hindu god of luck and protection
- Bes, an Egyptian god of protection and prosperity
- Jengu are mystical African origin creatures who are incredibly beautiful and bring luck to all who see them
- Felicitas, a Roman goddess of fertility, productivity, and good fortune

This altar charges your tools and surfaces, but more importantly, it charges your spirit with positive energy. The stronger your focus, the more successful your spells will be.

Before you cast any spells regarding wealth or prosperity, focus on improving your luck. Attracting good fortune should be part of your Hoodoo life and should be performed regularly.

A Simple Good Luck Spell

What You Need

- Three green candles
- Incense
- Three acorns

Place the candles into the form of a triangle and place an acorn at each one's base. Light your incense and candles simultaneously.

Recite the following

> *"Lady Luck and all her handmaidens, I ask for your assistance*
>
> *Give me the strength of a bear and the luck of a rabbit*
>
> *I summon the four elements to aid my work*
>
> *Bring me health and wealth and bring luck to all I do*
>
> *So be it."*

Once the candles have burned down, take the wax and wrap it in green silk before burying it beneath a fruit-bearing tree.

Another simple way to banish bad luck and bring good is to bring a rabbit's foot talisman or amulet to your altar. Place it in the center as you recite this phrase three times *"Bad luck run away from me, you're never welcome here, good luck fortune come to me, you're always welcome here."*

Sprinkle the rabbit's foot with lucky oils like chamomile or lemongrass as you throw a pinch of sacred salt over your left shoulder.

Carry the rabbit's foot with you whenever you feel the need to increase your luck.

How to Attract Wealth and Prosperity Using Hoodoo

The Money Spell

This basic candle spell should be performed over nine days for the most successful results. It can be performed any time of the day but should be repeated at the same time of day for the spell's duration.

What You Need

- A green candle

- A white candle

- Prosperity oil like bergamot, eucalyptus, or jasmine

In this spell, the green candle represents wealth and money, and the white candle represents you. To maximize the power of the spell, you can inscribe the white candle with your name.

Step 1) Charge your candles with the oil you have chosen

Step 2) Place them on your altar nine inches apart

Step 3) Light them both and repeat the following chant

> *"Money and wealth come to me*
>
> *In fullness and in plenty three times three*
>
> *I seek enrichment without harming none*
>
> *With your help, it will be done*
>
> *Money, I welcome you three times three."*

Step 4) Move the two candles one inch closer to each other

Step 5) Extinguish the candles

Step 6) Repeat the ritual for nine days

Step 7) On the ninth day, let the candles burn to wax before wrapping the remains in a white cloth and placing it in your mojo bag or wallet.

Spell for Business Growth

If you have a business, you know that hard work and long hours are all part of your success. You feel excited and nervous about your business and dedicate all your energy to your business growth dreams. No matter what you do and despite giving 100%, things can still become stuck. This is when you can turn to your Hoodoo learnings to give your business the boost it needs and restore your confidence in the future.

What You Need

- A large plate
- ¼ cup of curd
- Seven coins (include some foreign coins)
- Red mojo bag
- Fast luck oil
- Almond oil
- One green, yellow, red, and blue candle
- A small magnet

First, write the name of your business on a piece of paper and place it under the plate. If you don't have a name yet, write what your intentions and dreams for the business involve.

Carve the symbol of the sun on each candle and anoint them with your oils. Place the curd on top of the plate, then arrange the coins into the shape of a horseshoe. Place the green candle at the top of the plate, the yellow to the right, the blue to the left, and the red at the bottom. Place the magnet in the center of your candles, then light the green candle.

Pray to the gods and goddesses of plenty and ask for their assistance. Now light the yellow candle and repeat your prayers. Follow this with the red and blue candle.

Once the candles have burned down, take the remnants of the curd, the wax, and the coins and place them in your red mojo bag. Carry it with you wherever you go. The spell should be reenergized and repeated every six months or whenever you feel the need.

Remember, there are no freebies in business. All exchanges should be equal, and you need to keep yourself energized. This doesn't mean you can't be generous or helpful but don't overextend yourself or be overly generous.

The Green Candle Money Spell

This simple spell is popular and powerful. Use it to bring wealth and prosperity to your life. Remember, wealth isn't always about finances; it can also mean wealth, knowledge, or love. Good fortune is just as important as financial abundance.

What You Need

- A green candle
- Six coins, two gold, two silver, and two bronze
- A gold cloth
- Jasmine oil

Prepare your altar and take a moment to pray to your favorite deity. Ask for assistance in your magic work, and pray for success. Once you feel charged with energy, begin the spell.

Anoint the candle with your oil and place it in the center of your altar.

Place the six coins around the candle to form a circle of alternate-colored coins,

As you prepare the candle and coins, visualize what you will do with the money or good fortune your spell will attract.

Light your candle while repeating the phrase below three times

"Make the money flow and make my fortunes grow. As the money shines, god fortune will be mine."

Lay out the gold cloth and place the six coins on it. Form a pouch from the cloth while repeating this phrase

"Money comes three by three; all good fortune come to me."

Carry the pouch with you wherever you periodically charge it with your favorite herb or oil to make it work.

The Eight Day Money Bag Spell

Prepare your altar and your positive energies before you start the spell.

What You Need

- A green mojo bag
- Eight coins of different denominations (include foreign coins)
- Eight eucalyptus leaves
- Jasmine oil
- Citrine crystal

Place the coins on your altar and sprinkle them with some of your jasmine oil. Bless them by repeating this phrase eight times:

"Money grows on trees so that riches come to me."

Place the coins, leaves, and crystal in your bag, draw the string tight and bless the bag with the remaining oil.

Everything's Coming Up Aces Spell

What You Need

- An unopened deck of cards
- Breadcrumbs
- Sacred salt
- Silver candle
- Seven coins
- Any lucky metal talisman you love

Open the deck of cards and remove the four aces from the pack. Place them on your altar with the two red aces at north and south and the two black aces at eat and west.

Cover the aces with the breadcrumbs and sacred salt. Scatter the coins around your altar and then place the silver candle in a safe place.

Light the candle and bless your selected talisman before placing it on the altar.

Repeat this phrase three times:

> *"Aces high or aces low, money and luck to me will flow."*

Once the candle has burned down, use the wax to mark the four aces and place them in a safe place.

Dream Job Spell

If you find the cause of your money worries or financial strife is your job, then use this spell to change your career path and earn more money.

What You Need

- Piece of paper and a pen
- Peppermint oil
- Three cloves of garlic
- Silver coin
- Green mojo bag

Write a detailed description of your dream job on the paper. Include salary expectations and a full description of what your duties will be. Sprinkle the peppermint oil on the paper and place it in the bag.

Put the garlic and silver coin in with the bag and repeat the following phrase seven times

> *"Work and love go hand in hand, bless my life with both, help me find the best for me and let my career grow."*

Lucky 7's Ritual for Money and Success

We all know the power of numerology in our Hoodoo workings, and this ritual is a classic example of the strong associations connected to the number 7. Involve your friends and make it into a joint effort to improve everybody's finances.

What You Need

- Eight single dollar bills with 7 as their Federal Reserve number*

- 1 clear quartz crystal

- Iron pyrite stone (also called fool's gold)

- Aventurine quartz

*This number is part of the two-digit mark on each dollar note that indicates which bank it originates from. Seven is the number that refers to Chicago, and the 7 will come with a letter. You can choose dollars with a 7 as part of their serial numbers, but the spell won't be as effective.

Take your time to source your dollars and make your spell more potent. Also, the bills should come to you organically over some time. If you go to the bank and ask the teller to source your bills for you, the power of your spell will lessen. Acquiring the bills and showing patience will make you feel more powerful and enthusiastic about the magic you are about to create.

Begin by giving one of your bills to a friend and explaining what you are hoping to achieve. Use your social circle to create a powerful group who are all performing the ritual, and the power of your magic will increase.

Place the remaining seven dollars on your altar or in a silver money clip in a safe place and rest the crystals and stones on top of them. Leave them to charge for seven days.

As your friends begin to gift you with relevant bills, swap them for the bills in your original pile. This fresh injection of energy and magic will help you become even more prosperous and blessed with wealth.

The Full Moon Money Spell

The moon plays a huge part in magical rituals, so it wouldn't be right to omit a spell performed in the moonlight, enhancing its power. Perform this spell under the full moonbeam at midnight, and your spell will become more powerful.

What You Need

- Copper cauldron or similar vessel

- Silver coin

- Peppermint oil

- Sacred salt

Fill the cauldron half full of water. Add the sacred salt and peppermint oil. Place the cauldron directly below the moon's beam and let the lunar power charge the water for thirty minutes before you add the silver coin.

Now recite the following chant three times:

"Powerful lady of the Moon, bring me wealth and make it soon

Share the abundance that you bring and make my life with money ring."

Once the ritual is over, pour the water into the ground and thank it for its help. Place the silver coin in your pocket and keep it with you always.

The main thing to remember when attracting wealth, prosperity, and good luck to your life is to keep your energy levels high and filled with positivity. Use these spells in conjunction with protection powders and herbs to protect your home and yourself from negative forces.

Chapter 12: Daily Hoodoo Routines

No matter what your belief system is, it can be difficult to incorporate your practice into everyday life. Workplaces and other people's homes may not welcome you imposing your beliefs upon others, but that shouldn't mean you need to leave your beliefs at home. There are many ways you can bring your Hoodoo folk magic with you to protect you and bring you luck and love.

When we consider the origins of Hoodoo, it can be easy to forget these folks didn't have a great deal to work with. The slaves that heralded the more powerful aspects of Hoodoo often only had meager kitchen supplies, which they combined with working with the nature surrounding them.

Modern life means you have greater access to manufactured items produced to help perform rituals and spells to improve your lot. However, as with most practices, the old ways are often the most successful, so it is sometimes best to stick to the more traditional blends of herbs and oils to make the magic work.

Ways to Bring Hoodoo Into Your Daily Routine

Most homes have showers in their bathroom, while fewer have bathtubs. Lingering in a bathtub filled with scented water and bubbles is symbolic of luxury rather than everyday washing. So how do you bring the Hoodoo staple ritual of bathing in powders and oils into your life?

We all need to clean ourselves using shower gels or soap, so instead of taking a bath with herbal infusions, you can use soap or gel laced with powerful herbs and oils. The Art of the Root store has some amazing products, including the following.

- The Crown of Success Soap includes High John the Conqueror root, bergamot, vetiver, and other successful herbs and oils

- Come to Me Soap containing jasmine, gardenia, and other love relating herbs and oils for attracting romance and love

- Money drawing soap including cinnamon, chamomile, and other lucky herbs

You can make your own soaps and shower gels to use in your daily routine that your intent and magic will power. Start with an unscented base and add the oils and herbs you favor for a truly magical way to wash.

Having certain Hoodoo waters in your home will also enhance your powers. Florida, Moon, Orange, and Glory waters can be made and kept in your bathroom so you can anoint your body before you set out for the day.

How to Make Hoodoo Waters

The purest forms of blessed waters use rainwater or holy water as a base, while some use alcohol in varying forms. Then add the ingredients you require to make your water magical. Honey, salt, essential oils, and herbs can all be added to make your version of Hoodoo water.

Keep the waters in spray bottles clearly labeled with the type of power it holds. Spray it as you would room for freshening sprays. Anoint doors and windows to keep your house a powerfully safe place and attract good luck and prosperity.

A Typical Recipe for Florida Water

One of the most multi-functional waters available is Florida Hoodoo water

What You Need

- 17 ounces Vodka, cheap stuff works just and expensive, so don't waste the good vodka in your drink's cabinet
- Fresh mint
- Fresh basil
- Dried jasmine
- Dried lavender
- Lemon peel
- One cinnamon stick
- A clove
- Allspice berries

Place the vodka in a copper saucepan and heat it for 10 minutes on low heat. Add the ingredients and simmer for 40 minutes. Bottle when cooled and enjoy!

Florida water can be used as a cologne or perfume that smells great and is a powerful connection to your Hoodoo beliefs.

Your Mojo Bag and Why You Should Always Carry One With You

Your mojo bag is a highly personal piece of magic, so why would you leave it out of your daily routine? Although you need to keep it secret, there is always a way to carry it with you. Always keep a small version on your person and charge it with your favorite herbs and keepsakes.

Make bags for all occasions and keep them in your personal space. If you need protection or help with romance, choose the bag that will help you the most. Think of your mojo bag as an invisible force keeping you safe and improving your life.

State Your Intentions

Hoodoo doesn't rely on objects and rituals to work. These aspects of rootwork will enhance your magic, but your intentions are the most important part of your work. These fuel your soul and power your life, so it's important to get them out there into the world so they can be heard.

Never be afraid to state your intentions clearly and with a steady tone. If you feel your work is undervalued, then tell someone. Does your partner neglect the housework and rely on you too much? Tell them. You shouldn't have to rely on magic and spells to make your intentions come to fruition.

You can give them a helping hand with Hoodoo. Write down your intentions before you attend important meetings and use the paper to gain the upper hand. If you want a promotion, write down what your new title will be nine times on a piece of paper and wear it on your person when attending the interview.

Amulets and talismans are also a powerful way to carry your intentions with you. Carve a more permanent reminder of what you want on a stone or a piece of bark and carry it in your pocket. Paper intentions are okay for short-term intentions, but a stone or other natural materials work better in the long run.

Timing

We have already discovered how the moon and its position in the sky affect Hoodoo's work, but there are other considerations to ponder. The time of day is a key factor when performing your work and magic. If you perform a spell to repel things or diminish threats, perform your work as the minute hand is traveling down (e.g., from 12 o'clock to 12.30.) If your spell is to attract, then perform it as the minute hand travels upward (e.g., from 11:30 to 12 o'clock.)

Time is an auspicious part of Hoodoo, and when you bring that knowledge into your everyday life, you can draw energy from all aspects. The prime hours for Hoodoo work are 2, 9, 11, and 12 o clock, both in the am and pm, and the hours between 4 and 7 o clock. Schedule your day around these hours, and you will benefit from an increased sense of positivity and power.

Food and Drink Related to Hoodoo

When you think about your day and how to bring your beliefs to your home or life, then mealtimes must be considered. We all eat, and food helps us connect to other people and form bonds. Sitting at a family dining table sharing dishes with loved ones is a special experience. Sharing food with friends can make an ordinary get-together into a memorable time.

Bringing the essence of Hoodoo and folk magic to the table will help you connect to the ancestors and improve your links to those who practiced the craft before you. This can be as simple a process as adding some of those tasty herbs you use in magic to make your food taste better, or it can be full dishes that originate from slave roots and the concept of soul food.

Here are Some Herbs That are Guaranteed to Improve Your Food

- For love add bay leaves, cardamom, dill, and frangipani

- For protection, add anise, fennel, juniper, and rosemary

- For luck, add allspice, cinnamon, nutmeg, and orange

If you love to experiment in the kitchen, why not try some recipes that originate from the early Hoodoo communities. You will improve your taste buds and feed your soul.

If you fancy eating outside but are bored with the traditional BBQ dishes you regularly serve, try this seafood boil. All the family can get involved, and the history behind the dish will fascinate them. Back in the day, lots of people ate catfish and combined the fish with other commonly found seafood to create a huge pot of tasty food to feed their families and friends.

Seafood Boil

Ingredients

- 160 cups of water

- 2 sliced lemons

- 2 sweet onions

- 3 sprigs of parsley, thyme, and dill

- 8 small cloves of garlic

- ½ cup of salted butter

- 1 tbsp cider

- 2 tbsp garlic powder

- 2 tbsp salt

- 1 tbsp onion powder

- 1 tbsp dried oregano

- 3 lb. crab legs

- 2 lb. of prepared shrimp

- 1 lb. crabs' claws
- 4 lobster tails
- 2 lb. smoked sausage
- 8 corn cobs sliced into three parts
- 6 potatoes

Directions

1) Take a large pot capable of holding all your ingredients and place it on the stove

2) Check all the seafood and herbs are clean and free from shells and stalks

3) Chop both of your onions and both lemons and throw them in the pot

4) Add the water, herbs, garlic, butter, cider, and the dried ingredients to the pot

5) Boil the water and then reduce the heat to a medium setting

6) Cook for 45 minutes and then remove all the detritus from your herbs

7) Add the sausage, corn, and potato and cook for 15 minutes

8) Add all the seafood except the shrimp and cook for 10 minutes

9) Add the shrimp and turn the heat off

10) Let it sit for 10 minutes before serving

Take the pot out to the garden and serve it to your guests. Have plenty of newspaper or paper towels ready for cleaning your fingers, and then dig in! Let the kids and adults fish out the tasty claws and lobster tails and dip them in a garlic sauce or a zesty lemon sauce and accompany the dish with some traditional cornbread.

Cornbread Recipe

Ingredients

- 1 cup cornmeal
- 1 cup all-purpose flour
- 1/3 cup of sugar
- 1 tbsp baking powder
- ½ tsp salt
- 2 eggs
- ¼ cup of melted salted butter
- 1 cup full-fat milk

1) Preheat the oven to 400 degrees F

2) Prepare a greased dish or pan

3) Beat milk, eggs, and butter in a large bowl

4) Add remaining ingredients and mix until the batter is smooth

5) Cook for 20-25 minutes until the bread is a golden-brown color

You can add other ingredients to your bread to make it tasty. Jalapeno peppers and chili flakes are great if you prefer a kick with your cornmeal bread.

Hoecake

Legend tells us that enslaved people cooked these corn cakes on their hoes in the field as a mid-day snack. Some slaves had use of a griddle in the hearth called a hoe, while others baked them on a board facing their fires.

Ingredients

- 1 cup stone-ground cornmeal
- ¾ cup of boiling water
- ½ tsp salt

- ¼ cup of shortening, lard, vegetable oil, or beef tallow

1) Mix the salt and corn flour in a bowl

2) Melt the shortening in a skillet or frying pan

3) Take a tbsp of batter and add it to the hot fat

4) Fry until firm and light brown

5) Drain on paper towels before serving them warm with butter or honey

Sweet potatoes, okra, chitlins, and pigs' feet were stapled parts of Hoodoo fare, and they can be used to enhance your dining table today. Food is the perfect way to marry your beliefs with your everyday life.

Sweet Potato Casserole

This everyday filling dish is perfect for including all your favorite ingredients and herbs.

Ingredients

- 4 large, sweet potatoes
- 2 beaten eggs
- 4 tbsp butter
- ½ cup milk
- ½ tsp vanilla extract
- ½ cup all-purpose flour
- ½ cup crushed nuts to garnish
- ½ cup butter
- ½ cup sugar

1) Preheat the oven to 325 F while cooking the sweet potatoes in salted water for 15 minutes or until soft

2) Add the cooked potatoes to the milk, butter, and vanilla extract. Season to taste and add required herbs

3) Mix until smooth

4) Make the topping by combining the flour, sugar, and butter and add the nuts

5) Place the potato mix in a baking dish and top with the topping

6) Bake for 30 minutes until the top is crispy

What Better Than a Sweet Tea to Accompany Your Hoodoo-Based Food?

Here are some traditional sweet teas that are both tasty and healthy. The sweetness comes from the actual tea as opposed to sugar. The sweetness originates from the leaves and compounds in the roots of the plant and is a perfect way to bring Hoodoo roots to the table.

Rooibos

Also known as African red bush tea, this is one of the most versatile herbal drinks in the world. Drink it hot or cold and use it to make your favorite latte tastier and healthier. The sweet taste and lack of caffeine make it a perfect drink to serve children.

Licorice Root

This root-based tea is strictly for people with a real sweet tooth. Imagine candy melted in hot water that can be drunk guilt-free. That is what licorice root tea tastes like. Enjoy it as it comes, or add some of your favorite Hoodoo herbs to make the taste more personal.

Chamomile

One of the most available forms of herbal teas, not all brands taste the same. The best types of chamomile tea have a deep yellow hue with a subtle sweet taste.

Cinnamon

This tea is for people who prefer a spicier drink but don't mind a touch of sweetness. Source teas made from the bark of the plant for a more intense flavor.

Black Tea

If you want a sweet version of this mainly Indian type of tea, choose Chinese brands like Golden Monkey. The plants used for this tea have yellow buds that bring a hint of chocolate and honey to the brew.

Conclusion

So, now you know the power and magic contained in the learnings of Hoodoo. You can now attract love and wealth while protecting yourself against your enemies. Use your new powers carefully and always respect the guidelines that accompany the folk magic you use.

There are opportunities to misuse magic, and you can cause distress and pain to others, but you should be guided by your conscience and social conventions. You can bring happiness and love to your world and others, so concentrate on the good you can bring. Good luck with your magic, and remember to pay respects to the ancestors who formed the craft.

Here's another book by Mari Silva that you might like

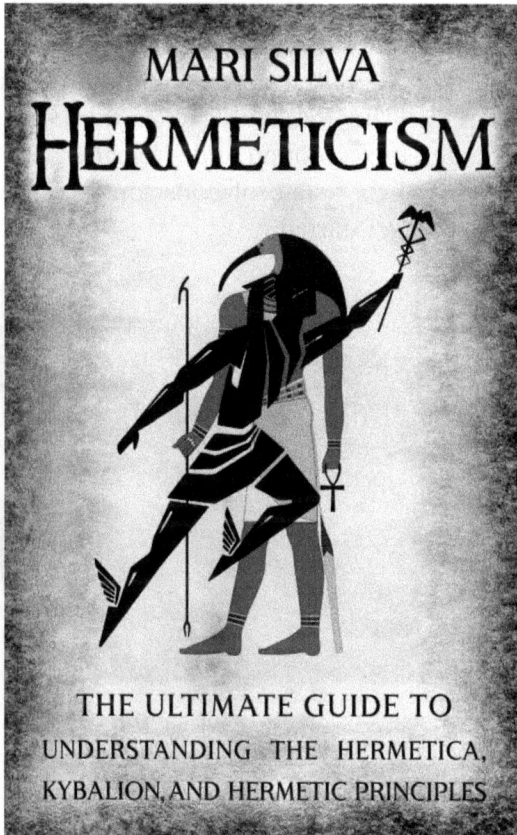

MARI SILVA

HERMETICISM

THE ULTIMATE GUIDE TO UNDERSTANDING THE HERMETICA, KYBALION, AND HERMETIC PRINCIPLES

Your Free Gift (only available for a limited time)

Thanks for getting this book! If you want to learn more about various spirituality topics, then join Mari Silva's community and get a free guided meditation MP3 for awakening your third eye. This guided meditation mp3 is designed to open and strengthen ones third eye so you can experience a higher state of consciousness. Simply visit the link below the image to get started.

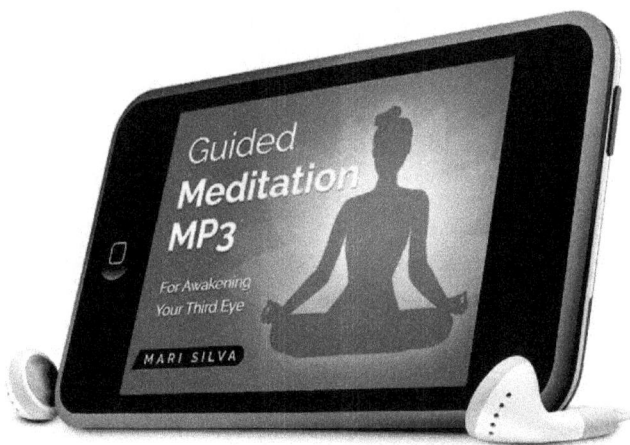

https://spiritualityspot.com/meditation

References

"11 Quick Cleansing Spells [for Your Spirit, House & Loved Ones]." Magickalspot.com, 2019,

magickalspot.com/cleansing-spells/.

"Augury Bird Divination: History & How to Read Bird Flight Patterns." Otherworldly Oracle, 2 May 2019,

otherworldlyoracle.com/augury-bird-divination-bird-flight-patterns/.

Candle Spells - Hoodoo Candle Rootwork | Conjure - Hoodoo - Witchcraft - Folk Magic. 22 July 2016,

www.southernfolkmagic.com/candle-spells/.

"Cleromancy - Throwing the Bones." The Bee Witch, http://www.mamabeewitch.com/mamabeesblog/throwing-the-bones.

Coles, Donyae. "Everyday Hoodoo: Washes, Mojo Bags, and Simple Charms." Spiral Nature Magazine, 30 July 2018,

www.spiralnature.com/magick/hoodoo-washes-mojo-bags-charms/.

---. "Four Hoodoo Rituals for the Full Moon and Beyond." Wear Your Voice, 3 Nov. 2017,

wearyourvoicemag.com/use-full-moon-anchor-hoodoo-rituals/.

Conjure, Doc. "The Demoniacal: The Hoodoo Truth: The Christianity of Hoodoo." The Demoniacal, 7 Jan. 2012,

thedemoniacal.blogspot.com/2012/01/hoodoo-truth-christianity-of-hoodoo.html.

"ConjureDoctor.com - Home of Dr. E. Hoodoo Products and Magical Services, Get What You Want!" Conjuredoctor.com, conjuredoctor.com/index.php.

Damian, Angel. "AMAZING: 7 Surefire Rituals to Bring Money Your Way." Themagichoroscope.com, 26 Nov. 2020, themagichoroscope.com/zodiac/money-spells.

"Dream Divination * Wicca-Spirituality.com." https://www.wicca-spirituality.com/, https://www.wicca-spirituality.com/dream-divination.html.

"Dream Divination Ritual." The Digital Ambler, 14 June 2019, digitalambler.com/rituals/dream-divination-ritual/.

Eirecrescent. "A Natural Witch- Grimoire of Life and Practice: How to Make Talismans and Amulets." A Natural Witch- Grimoire of Life and Practice, 23 May 2013, naturalwitchlife.blogspot.com/2013/05/how-to-make-talismans-and-amulets.html.

"9 Staples of Every Soul Food Menu." Flavors Soul Food, 15 May 2017, www.flavorssoulfood.com/9-staples-every-soul-food-menu/

"Full Moon Astrology." Carolina Conjure, https://www.carolinaconjure.com/full-moon-astrology.html.

"Herbal Roots 101: How to Prepare and Use Roots for Wellness." Herbal Academy, 27 Nov. 2018,

theherbalacademy.com/herbal-roots-101/.

Hollywood, John. "5 Money Spells, Rituals, and Chants to Attract Wealth." Exemplore - Paranormal, exemplore.com/wicca-witchcraft/moneyspells.

Hoodoo and Rootwork Roots – Black Magic Witch. blackmagicwitch.com/magic-herb-glossary/hoodoo-and-rootwork-roots/

"Hoodoo Candle Magic." Hoodoo Magic Spells, 18 Aug. 2020, hoodoomagicspells.com/hoodoo-candle-magic/.

"Hoodoo Curios and Supplies - Dr. E. Products." Conjuredoctor.com,

conjuredoctor.com/index.php?main_page=index&cPath=9.

Hoodoo Herbs – HoodooWitch. www.hoodoowitch.net/category/hoodoo-herbs/.

"Hoodoo, Rootwork, and Folk Magic: Olde Tales of the South." Otherworldly Oracle, 5 June 2018,

otherworldlyoracle.com/old-south-hoodoo-rootwork-folk-magic/

"Hoodoo Spells | EZ Spells." Www.ezspells.com, 29 June 2020, www.ezspells.com/hoodoo-spells/

Hoodoo Style Recipes - Black Witch Coven. blackwitchcoven.com/black-magick-spell-grimore/recipes-for-oils-incense/hoodoo-style-recipes/.

"How to Perform a House Cleansing in the Hoodoo Rootwork Tradition." Impact Shamanism, https://www.impactshamanism.com/blog/2019/1/18/how-to-perform-a-house-cleansing-in-the-hoodoo-rootwork-tradition

"Introduction to Hoodoo." Carolina Conjure, 2011, https://www.carolinaconjure.com/introduction-to-hoodoo.html.

"Lust Spells and Sex Magic." Wishbonix, 22 Sept. 2019, www.wishbonix.com/lust-spells/.

moodymoons. "The Ancient Art of Bone Reading for Beginners." Moody Moons, 29 Mar. 2019,

www.moodymoons.com/2019/03/29/the-ancient-art-of-bone-reading/.

"Recipes – Page 2." Hoodoo-Conjure.com, www.blog.hoodoo-conjure.com/category/recipes/page/2/.

Recipes: How to Prepare Different Hoodoo Powders – HoodooWitch. www.hoodoowitch.net/recipes-how-to-prepare-different-hoodoo-powders/

Sixth and Seventh Books of Moses – Occult World. occult-world.com/sixth-seventh-books-moses/.

"STEP-BY-STEP GUIDE on HOW to USE LOVE SPELLS." Www.hw-Group.com, www.hw-group.com/newsletter/list/how-to-use-love-spells.html.

"The Mojo." Carolina Conjure, https://www.carolinaconjure.com/the-mojo.html.

Universe, Voodoo. "Hoodoo House Blessing 101." Voodoo Universe, 14 Nov. 2017,

www.patheos.com/blogs/voodoouniverse/2017/11/hoodoo-house-blessing-101/.

[1]

---

[1]